ROME
AND THE VATICAN

280 PHOTOS IN COLOUR
MAPS OF THE TOWNS

FLORENCE

VENICE

BET
BONECHI EDIZIONI "IL TURISMO" FIRENZE

© Copyright 1998 by Bonechi Edizioni "Il Turismo" S.r.l.
Via dei Rustici, 5 - 50122 Florence
Tel. +39 (55) 239.82.24 - Fax +39 (55) 21.63.66
E-mail: barbara@bonechi.com / bbonechi@dada.it
http://www.bonechi.com
Printed in Italy

Photos: Bonechi Edizioni "il Turismo" S.r.l. Archives
          Rabatti and Domingie: pages 74 - 75 - 76 - 83 - 94 - 95 - 96
          K&B News: pages: 109 - 113 (at the bottom) - 118 - 133 (on top)
          I-Buga S.a.s. - Milano: pages 45 (Aut.SMA nr.0283/80) -
          113 (on top; Aut.SMA nr.710/87) - 117 (Aut.SMA nr.00034) -
          133 (at the bottom; Aut.SMA nr.000480) - 143 (Aut.SMA nr.000480)
Typesetting: Leadercomp, Florence
Reproductions: La Fotolitografia, Florence
Printing: BO.BA.DO.MA., Florence
ISBN 88-7204-075-2

INTRODUCTION

Rome, Capital of the World, Florence, a New Athens, and Venice, Bride of the Sea. All three definitions draw attention to the fact that the three towns are part of the heritage of the whole world and are not only the capital of Italy and two of its regional capitals. All three towns have played decisive roles in the history of the world and are objects of wonder, interest and admiration for the peoples of every country, religion and race.

Rome says the legend, was founded in 753 B.C. The Etrusco-Latin kings' city became a consular republic and then developed into the magnificent and flourishing capital of an immense empire, assembling the art and culture of the whole of the ancient Western world within its walls. The barbarians swept in from the east and north, mercilessly destroying all they could lay their hands on. But in time, Rome, as site of the martyrdom of the Vicar of Christ, assumed the spiritual leadership of Christianity and was filled with churches of every shape and description, which after almost two thousand years of history present an incomparable array of Christian architecture, ranging from the Basilica òf Saints Nereus and Achilleus, in the catacombs of Domitilla, to solemn St. Sabina, built under Pope Celestinus (422-432), to the vast complex of the Basilica of St. Peter, erected over the Circus of Gaius and Nero, where baroque magnificence overlays the severe Renaissance structures, which in turn, mask Romanesque spiritual simplicity or restless, crumbling Paleochristian Classicism. Centuries of history in fascinating layers. Before Rome, the cultural capital of the Western world had been Athens. When the sway of the Roman eagle was defeated, Constantinople inherited the Greek and Roman heritage. In 1453, after exhausting battles and sieges, the Pearl of the Bosphorus, the capital of the Eastern Roman Empire was finally taken by Mahomet II and his fearsome janissaries. The terrified scholars of Byzantium fled to the West, mostly to Italy, carrying with them centuries of culture and learning in their minds and books. Many of them had stayed in Florence — in 1439 — during the Council of Florence when King John VII Paleologus had attempted to promote the unification of the Churches of Byzantium and Rome so as to be able to summon up the western hosts against the Turk. In the Florence of the Council — already the Florence of the Medici, the scholars had found a stimulating climate, in which novel yeasts were bubbling; a renewed striving after classical certainty and harmony. When the capital of the Eastern Roman Empire finally capitulated to the Turkish crescent, its scholars returned to Florence to relight the torch of Greek and Roman learning and art, after it had nearly been brutally extinguished by the conquerors of Costantinople.

Florence, the next stage on our itinerary, the town of the lily, the flowered city, founded about 59 B.C., on the silvery river Arno by order of Julius Caesar, who had given his veterans the task of guarding and defending this fordable point of the river, surrounded by fertile, colonizable land. Florentia Tuscorum, as its Roman founders called it, dedicated to Flora, the fertile Spring goddess, by the white-haired followers of Mars — became an embattled city within the walls built for it by Arnolfo di Cambio at the end of the XIIIth Cent. The fierce pride of the walls echoed the menacing height of Arnolfo's great Palazzo della Signoria. Medieval Florence was a ferociously Guelph town, peopled by able merchants and refined art lovers. Literature, philosophy, architecture, sculpture and painting flourished in its busy streets. Influential merchant bankers, like the Medici, wielded the secret power of the Florentines, sagely setting up branches and warehouses all over the West, contracting alliances of every kind with the rulers and power-holders of all Europe. Thanks to the Medici family, Florence became a centre where the talents of painters, sculptors and architects were devotedly patronised. Lovers of beauty from the XVth century to the present have paid tribute to this town and will continue to do so, dazzled by the delights stored in it by Brunelleschi, Donatello, Michelangelo, Raphael, Pontormo, Bronzino and many others.

From the earth-bound beauty of Florence let us now move on to the evanescent marine grace of Venice. From Montaigne to Berlioz, from the English milords and Byron to Dostoevsky and Stendhal, no lover of beauty could travel through Italy without staying for a brief spell — at least — in St. Mark's pearly city on the lagoon. From Tuscany's cypresses and vines, one drives up the Italian peninsula and one gets to the dreamy Brenta valley. Venturing towards the lagoon, one steps into a world of light, in which sky and sea blend into each other and the mirage that is Venice lies etched against the horizon gleaming between the two luminous expanses. Venice was founded towards the middle of the Vth century A.D., after the arrival of the barbarians had obliged the people of the Brenta valley to take refuge on the islets of the lagoon. After building their first dwellings on wooden piles and platforms, thanks to their continuous contacts with the Exarchate of Ravenna, that remained for many centuries closely bound to the Byzantine traditions, the Venetians started venturing towards the eastern end of the Mediterranean, erecting their warehouses in ever more distant harbours and sailing back home with the wealth of the Middle East in their holds. The magnificent artistry of the mosaic layers and glaziers filled the vaults of the churches with splendour. In 1453 Venice and Genoa were the only western states to send ships and men to the rescue of Costantinople, so when the Capital of the Eastern Roman Empire collapsed, the Byzantine scholars not only migrated to Florence but to Venice as well, enriching the town with their learning and art treasures. Venice is the delightful result of this blending of east and west: a rich mixture of Byzantine and Gothic. The town's magic grace is inimitable and understandably celebrated by all its native painters: from Carpaccio to Canaletto and Guardi. Light transfigures all its buildings and St. Mark's, the Palace of the Doges, the Grand Canal and airy Santa Maria della Salute still gleem in all their lacy magnificence after centuries of floods and high water.

ROME

INDEX

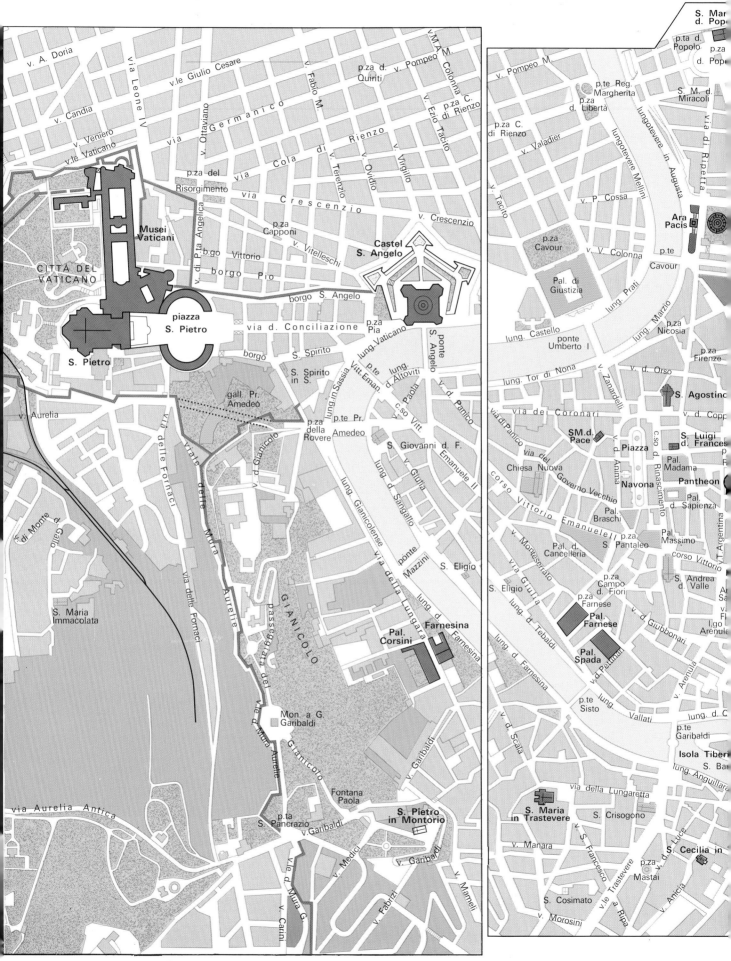

Pincio

Villa Borghese

Villa Medici

v. D'Annunzio

V.le di Muro Torto

V.le della Trinità

d. Monti

v. Margutta

via del Babuino

Trinità
d. Monti

piazza
di
Spagna

v. Vittoria
v. d. Croce

S. Carlo
al Corso

v. Condotti

v. Frattina

v. del Corso

Pal. Propag.
Fide

v. Due Macelli

S. Andrea
Fratte

v. F. Crispi

v. Sistina

v. Andrea
Fratte

p.za
S. Silvestro

ecitorio

l'go
Chigi

via del Tritone

Fontana
di Trevi

v. d. Dataria

Pal. d.
Quirinale

p.za
Colonna

v. d. Corso

v. d. Umiltà

Ignazio

Collegio
Romano

SS. Apostoli

Pal.
Colonna

p.za
di Pietra

Maria
nerva

Gall.
Doria-
Pamphilj

v. Battisti
p.za
Venezia

Foro
Traiano

Pal.
Venezia

v. XXIV Maggio

v. IV Novembre

eghe Oscure

Gesù

p.za
. Gesù

Vittoriano

Foro di
Augusto

v. d. Fori

p.za
Aracoeli

S. M.
in Aracoeli

S. Luca

Imperiali

Campidoglio

Foro Curia
Romano

Merc.
Traianei

Teatro
di Marcello

d. Teatro d'Ottavia

Nicola
in Carcere

vico
Jugario p.za d.
Consolazione

S. Giorgio
in Vel.

S. Teodoro

T. Portuno

v. di Marcello

T. Ercole

Arco di
Giano

Palatino

p.te
Palatino

S. Maria
in Cosmedin

v. del Circo

Lung. Aventino

v. d. Circo

S. Sabina

Circo Massimo

Massimo

via dei Cerchi

p.ta Salaria

c.so d'Italia

via Campania

c.so d'Italia

p.ta Pinciana

via Sardegna

via Spagna

via Piemonte

via Sicilia

P.ta Pia

via Veneto

via Sicilia

via Toscana

via Boncompagni

via Piemonte

via O. Sella

via P. Palestro

via Montebello

v. Ludovisi

v. Sallustiana

S. Maria
d. Vittoria

via XX Settembre

via Cadorna

v. S. Martino

Cappuccini

v. S. Basilio

v. Bissolati

v. A. Pastrengo

S. Maria
d. Angeli

Mus. Naz.
Romano

piazza
Indipendenza

v. Sistina

p.za
Barberini

via Barberini

p.za
S. Bernardo

via Montebello Goito

v. Voltturno

Solferino

v. d. Mille

Pal.
Barberini

v. d. Quattro

v. XX Settembre

via Torino

p.za d.
Repubblica

piazza dei
Cinquecento

v.le Castro Pretorio

S. Carlo

v. d. Fontane

via Nazionale

STAZ. F. S.
TERMINI

via Marsala

S. Andrea

v. d. Quirinale

v. Depretis

v. d. Viminale

v. Torino

via Amendola

via D. Principe Amedeo

via G. Giolitti

Pal.
Consulta

Pal. d.
Esposizioni

v. Palermo

v. C. Balbo

via Cavour

via F. Turati

Pal.
Rospigliosi

via Nazionale

v. d. Consulta

p.za
d. Esquilino

S. Maria
Maggiore

via Principe Amedeo

v. Milano

v. d. Serpenti

via Urbana

S. Prassede

v. Carlo Alberto

Villa
Aldobrandini

via Panisperna

via Cavour

via G. Lanza

via Merulana

p.za
Vittorio
Emanuele II

v. Baccina

S. Martino
ai Monti

Pal.
Brancaccio

v. Machiavelli

Foro
di Augusto

S. Pietro
in Vincoli

via del Monte Oppio

v. d. Termedi Traiano

p.za Dante

SS. Cosma
e Damiano Fori Imp.

v. d. Colosseo

v. d. Annibaldi

Terme
di Traiano

v. Mecenate

v. Merulana

Bas.
Massenzio

Domus
Aurea

v. G. Galilei

S. Francesca R.

T. di Venere
e Roma

via Labicana

via Bonghi

v.le Manzoni

Colosseo

S. Clemente

v. Labicana

v. T. Tasso

Arco di
Costantino

S. Giovanni
in Laterano

v. S. Giovanni

Domus
Augustana

v. Claudia

v. Capo d'Africa

SS. Quattro
Coronati

Scala San

Stadio

v. Celi Amon

p.za
Celimontana

Scala Santa

p.za S. Giov.
in Lat.

via di S. Gregorio

SS. Giovanni
e Paolo

Clivo di Scauro

S. Paolo
d. Croce

Arco di
Dolabella

v. S. Stefano Rotondo

S. Giovanni
in Laterano

S. Gregorio
Magno

p.za di
P.ta Capena

S. Maria
in Domnica

S. Stefano
Rotondo

ROME "CAPUT MUNDI"

The eternal city, *caput mundi* (capital of the world), *Urbs* (City) — these are some of the names people use to describe Italy's capital and largest city. A unique artistic-historical-religious center of over two thousand years of age, Rome has oft times been likened to Athens (the other great cradle of Western civilization). Nevertheless, it differs from the Greek city in one very important respect, for the visible remains of Rome's past are not confined to a single "historical section", but rather spread throughout her entire metropolitan area in a vital overlapping of periods and styles. Modern-day Rome, sprawling over a huge territory twenty miles from the Mediterranean, encompasses a million faces, some of which new (concrete and glass office buildings, housing developments, and midday traffic jams). Each district has its

keynote: shopping and eating out (Via Veneto, Via Condotti), antiques (Via del Babuino), art galleries (Via Margutta), genuine Roman spirit (Trastevere) — the list could go on and on. Rome is also a vital cultural center, boasting international universities and research centers, archives of unequalled value, a renowned opera house (Teatro dell'Opera) and music academy (Accademia Musicale di Santa Cecilia), as well as the prestigious Roman University. As a political capital, its history goes back two thousand years: centre of the Roman Empire, then of the Holy Roman Empire of the West, then of the United Kingdom of Italy, and finally of the Italian Republic. Some of the most salient aspects of Roman life are due to the fact that the capital of a modern state of about 60 million inhabitants hosts the offices of the President of the

Republic, of the Government, of the two Houses of Parliament, of the Ministeries and of the highest authorities of the Republic. Rome is also the headquarters of the Papal See. The Head of the Church is flanked by the College of Cardinals and by the Holy See. The city is moreover one of the most important pilgrimage centres (specially during religious festivities or when a Holy Year is proclaimed by the Pontiff). Rome is a blend of grandeur and chaos. The warm, ruddy tints of Baroque patrician mansions jostle with the gleaming travertine and marble columns of the Rome of the Caesars. The spacious sweep of piazzas and their welling fountains set-off the swelling grace of Borromini's church façades and soaring umbrella-pines stand etched against the sky-line on the hills surrounding the traffic-filled metropolis.

ROMAN FORUM

Situated at the junction of the Palatine, Capitoline, and Esquiline hills, the Roman Forum was for centuries the site of the city's most important public buildings (and thus of the city's major public events). The major sights include: the **Arch of Septimius Severus** (right), erected in 203 B.C. (the reliefs on its triple arch represent Rome's victories over Oriental tribes), the *Rostra*, or public speaking platforms, so called, because they used to be decorated with the rostrums (beaks) of captured war-galleys, the *Curia*, the brick Senate building, and the *Basilica Aemilia*, an immense Republican period building that rose alongside the Senate of which only little remains. On the Capitoline side: *Temple of Saturn* (eight granite columns and entablature) built in 497 B.C., the *Temple of Vespasian* (three corner Corinthian columns), and the *Portico degli Dei Consenti* (in honor of Olympus' twelve major deities) built in the 4th century A.D. and thus probably the last pagan monument in Rome. On the Palatine side: *Temple of Castor and Pollux* (three Corinthian columns) built in 484 B.C. to honour the warlike Heavenly Twins; the *Temple of Vesta*, a section of what was originally a circular colonnade of Corinthian columns); the *House of the Vestal Virgins* (of which several statues have survived; the Vestal priestesses were responsible for seeing that the sacred fire dedicated to the goddess Vesta never went out); the *Temple of Antoninus and Faustina* built in the 2nd century A.D. by the Senate in honor of Emperor Antoninus Pius and his wife Faustina (the building's original pronaos of six Corinthian columns has survived as the porch of the church of *San Lorenzo in Miranda*); the *Basilica of Maxentius*, an immense building begun by Maxentius and completed by Constantine (of the 35-meter-tall aisled building, two of the huge nave pillars have survived); and the *Arch of Titus* at the highest point of the *Via Sacra* that crossed the whole Forum, a one-arched triumphal gateway built to commemorate Titus' late 1st century A.D. defeat of the Jews. There are also some interesting churches by the Forum, including *Saints Luke and Martin* (Curia area) designed by Pietro da Cortona in the mid-1600s, *Santa Maria Nova* also known as *Santa Francesca Romana* (Basilica of Maxentius area), an 18th century church.

Starting from the left: in the middle, ruins of the **Basilica Emilia**, behind which is the **Temple of Antoninus and Faustina** incorporated into the church of San Lorenzo in Miranda. Moving toward the center, the *Decennales*, plinth of a column commemorating ten years of rule by Constantius and Galerius. Again in the middle, in front of the Temple of Antoninus and Faustina, are the remains of the foundations of the **Temple of Julius Caesar**, while in the

background, rises the Arch of Titus. To the right, almost in the middle, are the remains of the **Temple of Vesta** and of two honorary columns. Behind these rise three columns of the **Temple of Castor and Pollux**. In the background is the **Domus Tiberiana** on the Palatine Hill. On the extreme right, the **Column of Phocas**, and in the foreground, the base of the **Rostra**, named ofter their (lost) decoration of captured ship beaks, but actually an orator's podium.

IMPERIAL FORUMS

The first of the Imperial Forums, Caesar's, was built in 54 B.C. when the Roman Forum proved too small for the capital's ever-growing public activities. Trajan's, chronologically the last to be built, ranks as the largest. An entire medieval district was torn down to make way for the *Via dei Fori Imperiali* built in 1933 to traverse Rome's greatest archeological zone. Starting from Piazza Venezia, the first forum you encounter is *Trajan's Forum* built under the supervision of Apollodorus of Damascus, the renowned architect in the emperor's service from 107 to 114 A.D. The 35-meter-tall **Trajan's Column** (left) was built in 113 A.D. to commemorate the emperor's victory over the Dacians, probably by Apollodorus himself. It is adorned with a continuous relief that spirals approximately 200 meters around the column recounting **episodes from the war** (below). The statue of St. Peter on top was added in the 17th century (instead

of the original statue of Trajan). **Trajan's Market** (below right), three stories of shops and stores, once sprawled over the slopes of the Quirinal Hill (entrance from Via IV Novembre). Facing the marketplace was another of the Imperial *Forums, Caesar's*, which on three sides was surrounded by shops (*tabernae*), today little more than a heap of ruins. A section of entablature sustained by three Corinthian columns is all that remains of the **Temple of Venus Genitrix** (above), commissioned by Caesar in fulfillment of a vow made before the Battle of Pharsalus fought in 48 B.C. *Augustus' Forum*, situated alongside the marketplace, was girthed by a massive stone wall serving to isolate it from the frequent fires which broke out in the neighbouring working-class district of *Suburra*. The *Temple of Mars Ultor* (of which the base, some columns, and sections of cella wall are extant) was built to commemorate the Roman victory in the Battle of Philippi. Of *Nerva's Forum*, only fragments have survived. These include the so-called *Colonnacce* sustaining a remarkable frieze with a relief of women engaged in domestic pursuits.

COLOSSEUM

The Colosseum (actually the **Flavian Amphitheater**) ranks as Rome's greatest monument and the one which has become the symbol of the Eternal City itself. The enormous project was begun by Vespasian in 72 A.D. and inaugurated by Titus eight years later. It has been attributed to Rabirius, the architect of Domitian's Palace. It is elliptical in shape, its area measures 188 × 156 meters, and it is 57 meters tall. The four-story structure is wholly faced in travertine. The exterior consisted of three floors of eighty round arches in the Classical progression (Doric topped by Ionic topped by Corinthian) and an upper floor composed of a stone wall divided by pilaster strips with alternating windows. The opening was memorable as was the celebration held for the 1000th anniversary of the founding of Rome in 249 A.D. (hundreds of animals, including elephants, lions, tigers, hippos, zebras, and giraffes, as well as 2000 gladiators were killed). The shows comprised mock sea battles, tournaments, and games of all kinds in which death played a prominent part (despite the fact that no documentary evidence exists to back up the story of Christians being fed to the lions) and were open to all Roman citizens. Seating was on the basis of sex and social class. Performances continued well into the Christian era. (Gladiator fights were outlawed by Honorius in 404 A.D., although animal combats continued for another century). Throughout the Middle Ages, the Colosseum was used as a handy quarry. In addition, all the metal clamps between the facing blocks were removed over the centuries, leaving unsightly holes. The **subterranean chambers** where the animals were caged before the games may still be viewed inside (below and opposite page). Right: **model of the Colosseum** in the Museum of Roman Civilization; overleaf: **bird's-eye view** of the Colosseum.

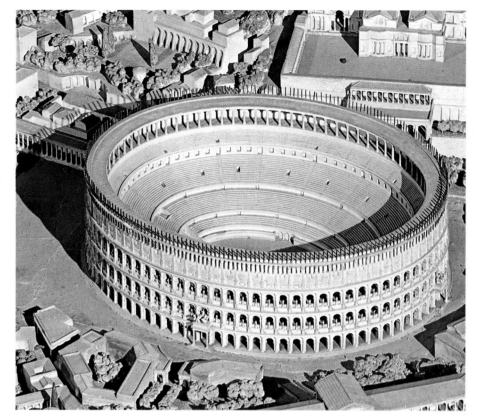

ARCH OF CONSTANTINE

One of the best preserved of the Roman triumphal arches, this celebrated monument embodies Rome's final artistic flowering which took place in the early 4th century A.D. It was built in 315 to commemorate Constantine's victory over Maxentius in the battle of Pons Milvius in 312. The 21-meter-tall, 25-meter-long triple arch contains statues and reliefs from pre-existing buildings, framed by immense Corinthian pillars: the eight *statues* of Dacians above the columns originally adorned Trajan's Forum, the *medallions* with hunting and sacrificial scenes date from the early 2nd century A.D., while the uppermost *reliefs* of battle scenes and imperial triumphs belonged to a building commemorating Marcus Aurelius. Nearby was the *Meta Sudans*, a cone-shaped fountain built by Constantine on the site of a previous fountain placed there by Titus in the 1st century A.D.

PALATINE

The hill believed by the Romans to be the site of Romulus' mythical founding of the city is actually, where the earliest settlements (9th-8th centuries B.C.) rose (above). Later it became an exclusive residential district (with a sumptuous imperial palace and numerous patrician villas). During the 16th century most of it was transformed into the Farnese family estate. Remains of Domitian's *Imperial Palace*, built in the late 1st century A.D. above pre-existing buildings, have survived. These include: the **Stadium** (right); *Domus Flavia*, and *Domus Augustana*, the majestic palace overlooking the Circus Maximus built as Augustus' private residence. Other sights on the Palatine include the *Temple of Cybele*, built in honor of the *Magna Mater* (Earth Mother goddess) the *House of Livia* (Augustus' wife), in which several frescoes have survived, and the *Circus Maximus*: the largest of the Roman circuses.

SANTA MARIA D'ARACOELI

The church rises on the spot where the Sibyl supposedly foretold the coming of the Son of God to the Emperor Augustus. A stairway leads up to the plain 14th century **façade** (above). Inside are some beautiful columns and fine 15th century works, including frescoes by Pinturicchio in the *Cappella Bufalini* (c. 1486) and tombs by Donatello and Andrea Bregno.

CAPITOLINE HILL

On the Campidoglio (or Capitoline Hill), the acropolis of ancient Rome, rose the temples of Capitoline Jupiter and Juno Moneta facing in the direction of the Roman Forum. Remodelled by Michelangelo in the 16th century, the square has since served as the city's political center (and today hosts Rome's city hall). The great ramp leads up to the remarkable *Piazza del Campidoglio*. At the far end is *Palace of the*

Senate which rises on the site of the *Tabularium* (Roman state archives). Apart from its fine external staircase (designed by Michelangelo himself), the palace was built between 1582 and 1605 by Giacomo Della Porta and Girolamo Rinaldi. The twin buildings leading up to it: *Palazzo dei Conservatori* on the right and *Palazzo Nuovo* (New Palace) on the left, were both designed by Michelangelo. Today they are museum buildings. In the center of the square is Michelangelo's base for the celebrated 2nd century A.D. equestrian statue of Marcus Aurelius.

CAPITOLINE MUSEUMS

Pope Sixtus IV bequeathed the first nucleus of the collection in 1471 (which makes this the oldest public collection in existence). It has been divided into three separate museums. The **Museo dei Conservatori**, one of the world's finest collections of Greek and Roman art, features sculpture, ceramics, mosaics, sarcophagi, etc. Its highlights include: *Apollo with a Bow*, a 5th century Greek original; a colossal statue of *Athena*, a copy of a 430 B.C. original by Cresilas; the so-called 1st century B.C. *Esquiline Venus*, and fragments of a *colossal statue of Constantine* (courtyard). The collection in the **Pinacoteca Capitolina** focuses mainly on 16th-18th century painting. Among the most noteworthy: Titian's **Baptism of Christ**, (right) dated 1512, Lorenzo Lotto's *Portrait of a Soldier*, c. 1522, Rubens' **Romulus and Remus being fed by the She-Wolf** (below), and Caravaggio's *St. John* and the *Fortune-Teller*, both youthful works. Several notable works adorn the rest of Palazzo dei Conservatori. In settings of frescoes, tapestries, and carved wooden ceilings are statues of *Urban VIII* by Bernini and *Innocent X* by Algardi, *Boy Removing a Thorn* (1st century B.C. bronze), and the celebrated Etruscan **Capitoline Wolf** (6th-5th century B.C.), a bronze statue of a she-wolf that has been the symbol of Rome for centuries (page 5). The figures of the twins were added by Antonio del Pollaiolo in the 15th century. The **Capitoline Museum** hosts another collection of Greek and Roman art. It contains some celebrated works such as the *Capitoline Venus*.

TRITON FOUNTAIN

This celebrated fountain, designed by Bernini in 1643, stands in the middle of bustling *Piazza Barberini*. It consists of a triton (merman) blowing a conch and standing on an open oyster which four dolphins hold aloft on their tails. The tails also bear the emblem of Pope Urban VIII Barberini who commissioned the project (photo above).

PIAZZA DEL POPOLO

The huge space between the *Porta del Popolo* (the old Flaminia Gate) and the meeting point of Via del Babuino with Via del Corso was designed in the early 1800s by Giuseppe Valadier, who combined old and new structures to create an unusually dramatic setting. On the south side are the twin churches of *Santa Maria di Montesanto* and *Santa Maria dei Miracoli* which were begun in the early 1600s by Carlo Rinaldi, and finished by Bernini some years later. Opposite them, Valadier erected two symmetrical buildings, one of which "conceals" a much older church, *Santa Maria del Popolo*. Important works of art are displayed inside the old church, among them two of Caravaggio's best-known paintings. The stairs leading to the top of the Pincio, was also designed by Valadier. The Egyptian obelisk, known as the *Flaminian Obelisk*, dates from the 12th century B.C.

TREVI FOUNTAIN

This enormous fountain alone occupies most of Piazza di Trevi, a charming square off Via del Corso. It rises on the spot where the Aqua Vergine, the aqueduct built by Agrippa in 19 B.C., had its terminus. After centuries of abandon, the aqueduct was reactivated when, in the 1400s, Pope Nicholas V commissioned Leon Battista Alberti to design a basin where its waters could be collected. The decorative elements (niches, sculpture, rocks, etc.) were added in the 18th century by Niccolò Salvi, who received the commission from Pope Clement XII. An imposing figure of the god *Oceanus* riding a gigantic seashell drawn by seahorses dominates the elaborate naturalistic-architectural setting in which other figures (tritons) loll among the rocks (left).

PIAZZA DI SPAGNA

The hour-glass shaped square is one of the most popular spots in the city. The fountain in the center of the square, the *Fontana della Barcaccia*, was designed by Pietro Bernini, father of the great Gian Lorenzo, in 1629. The stairs, the celebrated *Spanish Steps*, were built in 1726 by Francesco de Sanctis. At the top is an Egyptian obelisk, the so-called *Obelisco Sallustiano*, as well as a church, **Trinità dei Monti**, with a 16th century façade by Maderno (right).

TIBERINE ISLAND

The islet, dedicated by the Romans to the god of medicine, Aesculapius, was turned into a hospital (Ospedale di San Giovanni di Dio), in the 16th century. The church of *St. Bartholemew* opposite it was built in the 17th century. The nearby bridges are the *Pons Fabricius*, built in 62 B.C., the *Pons Cestius*, built in 46 B.C., and the 16th century *Ponte Rotto* (above).

PIAZZA NAVONA

This is a favorite haunt of Romans and non-Romans alike. Baroque in style, the oval square rises on the site of the *Stadium of Domitian* (above). The square contains three monumental fountains. The **Fontana del Moro** (right) was designed by Bernini (mid-1600s) and built by Antonio Mari. In the middle of the square is the **Fontana dei Fiumi** (lower right), one of Bernini's masterpieces. Dated 1651, it represents a cliff with the river gods of the *Ganges, Nile, Danube* and *River Plate* in dramatic attitudes seated around it. The third fountain, the *Fontana del Nettuno* originally lacked sculptural decoration. The figures of Neptune and seagods were added in the 19th century. Opposite is the church of *Sant'Agnese in Agone*, begun by Carlo and Girolamo Rainaldi in 1657.

PIAZZA DEL QUIRINALE

The setting of the square is splendid. It rises on the top of the Quirinal Hill, the site of the Roman Temple of Quirinus. The statues of Castor and Pollux, at the base of the Egyptian obelisk in the center, come from the Baths of Costantine. On one side of the square is the *Palazzo della Consulta*, the seat of Italy's Supreme Court. It was built by Ferdinando Fuga in 1734 as a courthouse for the *Tribunale della Consulta*. The coat-of-arms crowning the façade is the emblem of Clement XII who commissioned the building. The majestic **Palazzo del Quirinale** is the work of several architects, such as Mascherino, Fontana, Carlo Maderno, and Bernini (left). Begun in 1574, it was completed only around 1735. When Italy became a united kingdom at the end of the 19th century, it was used as the royal palace. It is now the official residence of the President of the Republic. Inside are works by Guido Reni and Melozzo da Forlì.

PANTHEON

This remarkable domed building has survived almost two thousand years of history virtually intact (left). The original rectangular temple built by Augustus' son-in-law Agrippa in 27 B.C. was turned into the pronaos of the present-day building when, in 120 A.D., Hadrian had it enlarged. The *pronaos* consists of sixteen ten-meter-tall columns, each topped by a Corinthian capital. The circular **interior** (right) has a diameter which is equal to its height (43.3 meters). The five-register lacunar *dome* rises to a central 9-meter-wide aperture. The building which the ancient Romans dedicated to the Pantheon (= all gods) became the burial place of Italian kings, queens and artists. Originally, gilded bronze adorned both the interior and exterior of the porch, but in the 17th century Pope Urban VIII Barberini had the facing removed so that Bernini could use it for the canopy he was constructing in St. Peter's (whence the Roman saying, "quod non fecerunt barbari, fecerunt Barberini" which being translated means, more or less: "where the barbarians failed, the Barberini prevailed").

SAN GIOVANNI IN LATERANO

The oldest church in Christendom, San Giovanni has been the Cathedral of Rome for almost 20 centuries. The striking **main façade** designed by Alessandro Galilei in 1735 marks the midpoint between Roman Baroque and neo-Classical (left). The **interior** was partially remodelled by Borromini in 1650 (below left). He redid the nave and double-aisle section, whereas the transept dating from the century before was left unaltered. The superb **tabernacle** in the transept is a mid-14th century work by Giovanni di Stefano (below right). One side of the church bears traces of wall dating from the High Middle Ages, whereas the belltowers were built in the 13th century, and the secondary façade was erected by Domenico Fontana in 1586. Detached from the church (entrance from Piazza San Giovanni in Laterano) is the *Baptistry*, whose origins date back to the time of Constantine.

SANTA MARIA MAGGIORE

Of the great basilicas of Rome, Santa Maria has best preserved its original Early Christian structure. Its 75-meter Romanesque *belltower* (dated 1377) is the tallest in the city. The five-arch **façade** was designed in 1750 by Ferdinando Fuga (above). Inside the loggia are superb mosaics originally part of the late 13th century façade. The stately single-aisle **interior** is lined with fine Ionic columns (right). It boasts considerable Cosmati floor mosaics (12th century) and a fine coffered *ceiling*. Its most remarkable feature, however, is its *mosaic decoration*: 36 panels from the 5th century (walls and nave arch) and others designed by Jacopo Torriti in 1295 (apse). The modifications and embellishments which have been added unceasingly over the centuries, and the many styles, crowding together, constitute a hamonious whole.

SAN PIETRO IN VINCOLI

The church is also known as the *Basilica Eudoxiana* as it was commissioned by Eudoxia the wife of Emperor Valentinian III in the early 5th century. The **chains** are those that bound St. Peter when he was confined in the Mamertine Prison in Rome miraculously fused with those that bound him in Palestine, still preserved inside the church (left). The five-arch porch was commissioned by Giuliano della Rovere and designed by Meo del Caprino around 1475 (above). The upper section of the *façade* whose only adornment consists of five windows, was built in the 16th century. St. Peter's is renowned for another reason — the great marble **Moses** carved by Michelangelo (right) in the right transept. It was carved for the *Tomb of Julius II*, the Della Rovere pope, which was supposed to be much bigger, having been conceived for St. Peter's in the Vatican. Michelangelo spent three years on the project, but the tomb as we see it was completed by pupils. The figure of Moses enthroned in the lower part of the monument is, however, by Michelangelo.

SAN PAOLO FUORI LE MURA

The second largest basilica in Rome was founded in the 4th century on the site of St. Paul's tomb (above left). Remodelled over the centuries, it was completely destroyed in 1823 and subsequently rebuilt. The huge building (132 × 65 meters) is preceded by a great *columned porch*. The five-aisled *interior* is adorned with a frieze of *mosaic portraits of popes*. The majestic **triumph arch** (above) at the end of the nave is a fairly faithful replica of the original, and the mosaics are original (albeit restored). The arch was called the Arch of Galla Placidia as it was supposedly commissioned by the Byzantine empress. A notable *ciborium* crafted by Arnolfo di Cambio in 1285 and the *apse mosaic* recall the artistic quality of the lost medieval church. The remarkable **cloister** is partially attributed to Pietro and Nicolò di Angelo Vassalletto.

SANTA MARIA IN COSMEDIN

The Romanesque church was founded in the 6th century (and rebuilt in the 12th). Inside are notable Cosmati school works: the floor, a canopy, and a *schola cantorum*. In the portico is the stone mask known as the **Bocca della Verità** (literally, mouth of truth), a marble disk representing a face, which probably served as a drain plug. According to popular belief, a liar who dares put his hand in the mouth will have it bitten off (photos on top and above right).

SANTA CECILIA IN TRASTEVERE

The original church was founded before the 5th century on the site of a Roman dwelling (perhaps the home of Cecilia, a 2nd century Roman martyr). Remodelled by Paschal I in the 9th century, it has since been rebuilt and redesigned several times (right). In the vestibule is the 15th century *Tomb of Cardinal Forteguerri* by Mino da Fiesole, while in the choir are two celebrated sculptures: Arnolfo di Cambio's *Ciborium* (1283) and Stefano Maderno's *St. Cecilia*. Perhaps the most celebrated of all is the Last Judgment fresco in the adjoining convent, with the portrait of *Christ the Redeemer*, painted by Pietro Cavallini in 1293; it is unfortunately now in poor condition.

SAN CARLINO ALLE QUATTRO FONTANE

Located at the intersection of Via del Quirinale and Via delle Quattro Fontane, this church is consecrated to the Holy Trinity and St. Charles Borromeo. Since it is very small, the Romans call it by a nickname (San Carlino). It was designed by the great Northern Italian Baroque artist, Francesco Borromini, whose Roman career began and ended right here. The unusual plan of the church was drawn up in 1638. It was the first time that Borromini, who up to then had always collaborated with Carlo Maderno, worked on his own. His design was quite original as he based it upon the proportions of a plinth from one of the great pillars in St. Peter's. The curving **façade** (left), on the other hand, was the last project carried out by the artist, who committed suicide in 1667. Other original features are the *dome* and *lantern*. The striking decoration of the interior (marble pillars, gilding, stuccos) was wholly designed by Francesco Borromini.

SAN PIETRO IN MONTORIO

The tiny round building (left) stands in the courtyard of the church of San Pietro in Montorio on the Janiculum Hill. San Pietro is a reconstruction of a 9th century church built above the spot where. St. Peter was supposedly crucified. The remodeling was sponsored by Ferdinand and Isabella of Spain towards the end of the 15th century. The little temple, on the other hand, is a pure Renaissance creation. It was designed by one of the greatest early Renaissance architects, Donato Bramante, who finished it in 1510. The domed building with its sixteen Doric columns, trabeation, and open gallery is Bramante's interpretation of the Classical style. Later, he would utilize a similar plan in his design for the reconstruction of St. Peter's which, was never actually built. The decoration of the building consists solely of marble flooring, whose inlay pattern recalls Cosmati motifs, and some 17th century sculpture. The grate in the lower level crypt marks the spot where St. Peter's cross supposedly stood.

SANTA MARIA IN TRASTEVERE

Reputedly founded by Pope Julius I around the year 340, Santa Maria in Trastevere is definitely one of the oldest churches in Rome, and the first known church dedicated to the Virgin. Like many others, it was remodelled and restored over the centuries, although the greatest damage was done in the 19th century when mediocre murals were painted on the walls and figures believed to be pagan were re-moved from some of the capitals. In 1702, Carlo Fontana was commissioned by Pope Clement V to add the imposing *porch* which covers the original 12th century **façade** with a 13th century mosaic by Pietro Cavallini (above). The statues atop the railing are 16th century, while the belltower still retains much of its 11th century Romanesque appearance. The same juxtaposition of styles and centuries is repeated inside the church. Of note are the mid-12th century *mosaics* decorating the apse. Those recounting *episodes from the life of Mary* were designed by Pietro Cavallini, about whom we know very little, and whose works have mostly been lost. Nevertheless, from what has survived, it is easy to see the reason for Cavallini's renown. In fact, he was also greatly admired by his contemporaries, among them Giotto.

VIA APPIA ANTICA

The famous road dates back to the beginning of Roman history. It was lengthened until it reached Brindisi (on the east coast), a major port for trade with the Orient. Originally, the road started from Porta Capena (hardly any of which is extant today). When the Aurelian Walls were built, its starting-point was moved to the Porta Appia and later it was moved again to Porta San Sebastiano. The Appian Way is the best-preserved of the consular roads — some of its paving even dates from Roman times. The first few miles are dotted with tombs and remains of monuments. Among the ruins that have been identified, the most noteworthy is undoubtedly the **Tomb of Cecilia Metella**, a round travertine structure built as a tomb for the daughter of Quintus Metellus (left).

CATACOMBS

The catacombs or "*coemeteria*", i.e. dormitories, were the burial places of the Christians. All catacombs were outside the walls of the city, as there was a law forbidding the burial of bodies within the precincts of the town. The ***Catacombs of Domitilla***, also known as the catacombs of St. Nereus and Achilleus, are among the largest in Rome. Perhaps they were used as the private burial grounds of prominent Christians, among whom Domitilla who, as niece of the Emperor Domitian, belonged to the imperial family of the Flavians. In the catacombs is the 4th century **basilica of Saint Nereus and Achilleus** a three-aisled church with superb Corinthian columns (left). The most noteworthy tombs include the *Hypogeum of the Flavians* with Ist century A.D. murals and the *Cubicle of St. Petronilla*. Only a tiny part of the ***Catacombs of St. Callistus***, also along the Appian Way, has been explored up to now. Built in the 2nd century A.D. on four levels, they served as the official burial grounds for the first bishops of Rome. The *Crypt of the Popes* contains the tombs of several pontiffs including that of Sixtus II, murdered in the persecutions of the Emperor Valerian in 258. On the opposite page: the **Crypt of St. Caecilia** (above); a **corridor** (below right) and a detail of a 6th century **fresco** (below left).

BORGHESE GALLERY

This unique private collection, housed in a charming 17th century building — the *Casino Borghese* — became property of the Italian state in 1902. Ground floor (sculpture): **Paolina Borghese** (Napoleon's sister) portrayed as Venus Victrix, Canova's celebrated sculpture of 1805 (above). One of the foremost masterpieces of neo-Classical sculpture, it is also a tour de force of the master's incredible technical skill. **David**, by Bernini, the face is a self-portrait of the master, 1624, (left); **Apollo and Daphne**, 1624 (above right opposite page) and **Rape of Persephone** (above left opposite page), another youthful work by Bernini (1622). Upstairs: paintings by Raphael (*Deposition*, dated 1507), Caravaggio (*Boy with a Basket*, *David with the Head of Goliath*, **St. Jerome**, (detail, below right) and the celebrated *Madonna dei Palafrenieri* painted in 1605-1606). The *St. Jerome* is one of Caravaggio's last works. The saint, sunk in

deepest thought is portrayed as a time-worn, wrinkled old man whose forehead is even more wrinkled from the strain of his intense mental effort. In 1606, Caravaggio, revolutionary in art, rebellious in life, was forced to flee Rome when he got involved in a violent tavern brawl that ended with the killing of a rival. After four years of restless wandering about Italy he died, half crazed, and feverish on the beach of Porto Ercole of an attack of malaria. See also Titian's *Sacred and Profane Love* and Antonello da Messina's *Portrait of a Gentleman*.

NATIONAL MUSEUM OF VILLA GIULIA

The museum was founded in 1889 as a collection of pre-Roman sculpture and artefacts from Latium (the province of Rome) and housed in Pope Julius III's 16th century villa. Shortly afterwards, it was expanded to include the Etruscan works from the Barberini, Castellani, and other collections. In the 1950s it was completely renovated in keeping with the most advanced museum criteria. The highlights include: a reconstructed *tomb from Cerveteri* (6th century B.C.), *Apollo* and *Heracles*, late 6th century B.C. Etruscan statues from Veii, and the **Sarcophagus of the married couple**, a remarkable Etruscan terracotta dating from the 6th century B.C. unearthed at Cerveteri (left). In addition there are dozens of bronze figurines and ceramic vases, including a 5th and 4th century B.C. vase, a 7th century B.C. *oinochoe*, several *ciste* (typical of the Palestrina area) among which is the superb 4th century B.C. *Ficoroni Cista*.

GALLERIA DORIA PAMPHILJ

One of the world's major private collections, it was started in the 17th century by Pope Innocent X Pamphilj, continued by his descendants, and, when the Pamphilj line died out, by the Doria family. It is housed in a grandiose Rococo mansion, *Palazzo Doria*, with a Renaissance courtyard. Most of the works are still hanging in the places selected by the original collectors; many are famous masterpieces (left). Among the Italians: Titian (*Spain Coming to the Aid of Religion* and *Herodiad*), Tintoretto, Correggio, Raphael (*Double Portrait*), Caravaggio (*Mary Magdalene, St. John,* and *Rest on the Flight into Egypt,* a youthful work still a long way from the shockingly realistic treatment of his mature works), Carracci, Savoldo, Mattia Preti, Parmigianino, and Salvator Rosa. Among the foreign masters, the most important are Velazquez (*Portrait of Innocent X,* dated 1650), Claude Lorrain (five *mythological landscapes*), Rubens (*Portrait of a Franciscan Monk*), Metsys, and Breughel.

ROMAN NATIONAL MUSEUM

The museum building was once a monastery. It contains some of the greatest Greek and Roman masterpieces. Among the most important works are: the *Athena Parthenos*, a Roman copy of Phidias' original 5th century B.C. Parthenon statue, *Galatian about to commit suicide after having killed his wife*, a copy of a Pergamon bronze (3rd century B.C.); the so-called *Ludovisi Throne*, an extraordinary 5th century B.C. work; the **Tiber Apollo** (above right), a Roman copy of a 5th century Greek original, attributed to Phidias or Kalamis; the *Lancellotti Discobolos*, copy of the famous statue by Myron, *Niobe's Daughter* from the Sallustian Gardens, copy of a Greek mid-5th century B.C. original; **Boxer at Rest**, (above left), an original Hellenistic bronze signed by Apollonius, the *Sacrifice of Augustus*, one of the finest Roman sculptures extant; *Sleeping Hermaphrodite*, copy of a Hellenistic original, as well as the celebrated *frescoes* from Livia's house at Prima Porta (1st century B.C.).

PALAZZO VENEZIA

It is the first example of Renaissance architecture in Rome. We know that the building was commissioned by Cardinal Pietro Balbo (later Pope Paul II) but the name of the architect who designed it in 1455 has not come down to us, although it is sometimes attributed to Leon Battista Alberti, known to have been working for Pope Nicholas V in Rome at the time. Thereafter, in the 16th century, it became the seat of the Embassy of the Republic of Venice. In the 19th century, it was taken over by the Austrians, and was not restored to the Italian government until 1916. Since the end of World War I, it has been a museum (**Museo di Palazzo Venezia**, shown on the left). Its superb collections include silver, ceramics, tapestries, paintings, and sculpture.

PALAZZO BARBERINI

A lovely Baroque palace, commissioned by Urban VIII (in 1624), begun by Carlo Maderno, continued by Borromini, and completed by Bernini (in 1633). It houses the 13th to 18th century section of the **National Gallery of Ancient Art**. The painters represented include: Simone Martini, Fra Angelico, Filippo Lippi, Raphael, El Greco, Tintoretto and Caravaggio. Right: la **Fornarina** by Raphael (1516).

ARA PACIS AUGUSTAE

The temple was commissioned by the Senate of Rome to commemorate the *Pax Augustae* (Peace of Augustus) proclaimed by Augustus throughout the empire in 14 B.C. It consists of a sacrificial altar around which is an enclosure adorned with *ornamental friezes* surmounted by stupendous *reliefs of processions* (left). Inaugurated in 9 B.C., it was gradually submerged by accumulated earth and rubble. Every so often, from the 16th century on, bits and pieces came to light. In 1939 G. Moretti put them all back together. Plaster casts were used for the few missing parts.

CASTEL SANT'ANGELO

This massive building, which looks like a medieval castle, rises on the site of *Hadrian's Mausoleum*. Most of the original floorplan and sections of the original building have survived (above). Built in 130 A.D. as the emperor's tomb, it had an immense square base on top of which was a circular drum structure. Then, in 271, Aurelian had it remodelled as a fort. Its name, literally, Castle of the Holy Angel, dates from 590 when an angel foretelling the end of a terrible plague epidemic reputedly appeared on its summit. Throughout the Middle Ages, it served as the popes' stronghold-prison, providing convenient shelter in the case of enemy attack. In the 15th century the great corner bastions were added on and the drum, devoid of its marble facing, was raised. A statue of the **angel** was set up to replace of one of the emperor on top of the building (left). (The present-day angel is an 18th century work). The vast five story *interior* is an intricate

labyrinth of rooms and corridors dating from various periods. Among the most interesting sights are the *spiral staircase* leading to the emperors' burial chamber preserved virtually intact, the *Courtyard of the Angel*, a picturesque medieval courtyard still containing medieval ammunitions, and the *Armoury*, containing an extensive collection of weapons from various places and periods. Another interesting section is the *Papal Suite*, which was remodelled and sumptuously refurbished by Baccio da Montelupo, Perin del Vaga, and other 16th century masters who received the commission from Pope Paul III.

THE VATICAN CITY

The Vatican City covers the Vatican Hill lying between Monte Mario and the Janiculum. In the 1st century B.C. it was the site of Caligula's circus — where Nero had hundreds of Christians martyred some years later. The church rises on the spot where one of Nero's victims, St. Peter, was buried. The Vatican, an independent state as from the 8th century, was of primary importance throughout the Middle Ages. The Papal State expanded to such an extent that, up to the unification of Italy, when it was wiped off the Italian political scene, it covered pratically all of Central Italy. It only regained an independent political status in 1929, as a state with less than a half a square kilometer of territory, under the terms of the Lateran Pact agreement signed with the Italian government, comprising the Basilica of St. Peter's, the great Square and the Vatican complex (photos above).

PIAZZA SAN PIETRO

Bernini created a striking scenic effect by enclosing the square inside a gigantic, four-pillar-deep colonnade. The uninspiring boulevard leading to the square, *Via della Conciliazione*, was built in 1937. Bernini worked on the *colonnade* which flanks two sides of the perfectly elliptical shaped, 240-meter-wide open space between 1656 and 1667. It is composed of 284 pillars surmounted by 140 *statues of saints and martyrs*. On either side are grandiose *fountains* designed by Carlo Ma-

derno. The Egyptian *obelisk* in the center, brought to Rome from Heliopolis by Caligula to adorn his circus, was set up on its present site in 1586 — an undertaking so arduous that, according to the records, it took over four months and required the efforts of over one thousand men and beasts of burden. During the Middle Ages, it was believed that the urn inside the golden sphere atop the obelisk contained the ashes of Julius Caesar (actually there is a relic of the Cross).

BASILICA OF ST. PETER'S

The greatest church in Christendom originated in 324 as a shrine for the mortal remains of St. Peter. The building we see today took hundreds of years to complete. The earliest version of the basilica had a five aisle plan with a façade characterized by a porch and mosaic decoration. In the 15th century, when landslides threatened the building's stability, Nicholas V had it torn down, at the same time commissioning Bernardo Rossellino to design a new one. When Nicholas V died, work was suspended and the project was not resumed until 1506 when Bramante, commissioned by Julius II, began working on his design based on a Greek cross. Bramante — who never completed his project — was succeeded by Raphael, Antonio da Sangallo, Peruzzi, and Michelangelo. Michelangelo designed the *dome*, the biggest ever built, in 1547, basing himself partially on Bramante's own plans and partially on Brunelleschi's dome on the Florence cathedral. (It was finished, however, sixteen years later by Domenico Fontana and Giacomo Della Por-

ta). In the 17th century, Carlo Maderno was commissioned to enlarge the church, which he did by lengthening the nave — thereby reshaping the ground plan into a Latin cross. Maderno's imposing **façade** was erected in 1614. A porch decorated with statues of popes precedes the church proper, which has five entrance portals. The one on the far right, the **Holy Door**, (right), is opened only on occasion of Holy Year celebrations, the middle one, the *Filarete Door*, boasts superb bronze reliefs cast by Filarete in 1433, while the one on the far left, the *Death Door*, is the work of a contemporary Italian master, Giacomo Manzù (1964). The **interior** conveys an impression of remarkable harmony despite truly gigantic dimensions (length: 210 m, width at the transepts: 137 m., height at the nave: 44 m., dome height: 136 m.). Eight pairs of immense pillars line the nave (following page, above left). By the last one on the righthand side is a **bronze effigy of St. Peter** (following page, below left). The much-venerated statue, dated around the middle of the

13th century, has been attributed to Arnolfo di Cambio. In the left aisle is the *Tomb of Innocent VIII* by Antonio del Pollaiolo (1498), while opposite, in the first chapel on the right aisle is Michelangelo's **Pietà** (opposite page). Sculpted when the master was only twenty-five years old for a French prelate, it is the sole work that bears his signature. Beneath the *dome* (which can be climbed) are the *Pope's Altar* and Maderno's *Chapel of the Confession*, i.e., a semicircular area surrounded by an altar rail where ninety-nine perpetual lights are kept burning above **St. Peter's Tomb** (above right).

Above the altar is the impressive bronze *Canopy*, to which Bernini gave the shape of a processional canopy (in lieu of the more traditional ciborium) sustained by oversize twisted columns (1624-1633). In the tribune is another of Bernini's striking Baroque creations, the gilded bronze **Throne of St. Peter** 1656-1665, (top right), flanked by two superb tombs. On the left is the *Tomb of Paul III* designed by Guglielmo Della Porta in 1575, while on the right is Bernini's *Tomb of Urban VIII* dated 1646. Four colossal statues adorn the dome pillars. (The *St. Longinus* holding a spear is also by Bernini.) In the

right transept is the *Tomb of Alexander VII*, dated 1678. In the adjoining chapel is a fine marble altarpiece depicting *St. Leo's encounter with Attila* sculpted by Algardi in 1650. Other notable works are preserved in the **Museum** and **Treasure-vault of St. Peter's**. The most significant include: a *ciborium* by Donatello (1432), the *Tomb of Sixtus IV*, a masterpiece of Renaissance sculpture executed by Antonio del Pollaiolo in 1493, and the *sarcophagus of Junius Bassus*, (4th century). In the underground chambers, the so-called **Grotte Vaticane**, are tombs of popes, sarcophagi, and other monuments.

VATICAN MUSEUMS

The incredible Vatican collections occupy a complex of buildings comprising over 1400 rooms and 20 courtyards. **Museo Pio Clementino**, containing the highlights of the Vatican's Greek and Roman collection, includes: the celebrated *Belvedere Torso*, perhaps representing Hercules, a late 1st century B.C. work by Apollonius of Nestor which was unearthed in the 15th century and was much admired by Michelangelo; *Meleagrus*, a Roman copy of a 4th century B.C. sculpture by Scopas; *Apollo killing a lizard; Satyr at rest*, and *Venus of Cnidus*, all Roman copies of Praxiteles, 4th century B.C. originals, **Sleeping Ariadne** (below right) a refined 2nd century B.C. Hellenistic work; the *Wounded Amazon*, Roman copy of a Phidias original (5th century B.C.); the **Laöcoon** (left), a celebrated marble group dating from the late Hellenistic period which came to light in the Domus Aurea (1st century B.C.); the extraordinary *Belvedere Apollo*, a Roman copy of a 4th century original by Leocares, and *Athlete grooming himself*, a Roman copy of a 4th century B.C. Lysippus. The **Chiaramonti Museum**: two great masterpieces, the *Prima Porta Augustus*, a late 1st century B.C. Roman work, and the *Spear-Holder*, a Roman copy of a 5th century B.C. Polycletus.

The **Vatican Picture Gallery**: the collection includes: Giotto's *Stefaneschi Altarpiece*, commissioned in 1300 for the main altar of the old basilica of St. Peter's, a painting by Fra Angelico (*scenes from the life of St. Nicholas*, predella), Melozzo da Forlì's **Sixtus IV and Platina** (right), detached fresco, and the celebrated **Music-Making Angels** (opposite page, below left); paintings by Raphael: the *Virgin of Foligno*, 1513, commissioned as an ex-voto offering by a prelate in the entourage of Julius II, the **Transfiguration** (below center), Raphael's last work and by some judged his finest, dated 1520, and the *Coronation of the Virgin* with its predella which, instead, is the first work the master, aged twenty, painted on his own (1503). Leonardo's unfinished *St. Jerome* that is nevertheless a remarkably effective painting; Giovanni Bellini's **Pietà** (c. 1474), which is the upper section of the Pesaro Altarpiece (below left). Works by Veronese, Titian (*Virgin and Child with saints*), Paris Bordone (*St. George and the Dragon*), Annibale and Lodovico Carracci, Federico Barocci, Guercino, Domenichino (*Communion of St. Jerome*, dated 1614), Guido Reni (*Crucifixion of St. Peter*), Caravaggio, the moving **Deposition** of 1604 (below right), van Dyck, Pietro da Cortona, Rubens, Poussin; portraits by Titian (*Doge Niccolò Marcello*), Thomas Lawrence (*George IV of England*), Carlo Maratta (*Clemens IX*), and others.

RAPHAEL'S STANZE

The apartments known as *Stanze* were begun under Nicholas V in the 15th century. In 1508, Pope Julius decided it was time to complete the decoration of the rooms, which had since been suspended, and called in famous artists such as Signorelli and Lorenzo Lotto. When work was already in progress, the Pope heard about a talented young painter, Raffaello Sanzio, from Bramante, like Raphael, a native of Urbino. Raphael was summoned to Rome and Julius was so impressed with the youth's trial piece, he fired everyone else and awarded him the commission. The **Stanza dell'Incendio di Borgo** shows *Pope Leo IV miraculously putting out a fire in the Borgo district.* However, the most famous frescoes, the **Disputation of the Holy Sacrament** (centre left) the **School of Athens** (below left) and **Parnassus** (above) are in the **Room of the Signature**. Whereas the *Disputation* represents the glorification of Catholicism, the *School of Athens*, which shows the greatest philosophers of all times portrayed around Plato and Aristotle, represents the triumph of philosophy. *Parnassus* represents the world of art. Around Apollo and the Muses are Dante, Virgil, Homer, and other great poets.

SISTINE CHAPEL

The conclave of cardinals meets to elect the new pope beneath Michelangelo's stirring frescoes (general view page 53). The earliest frescoes, those along the walls, date from 1481. They recount the **life of Moses** (above right page 56) and **Christ** (above left and below page 56) in twelve panels painted by some of the major figures of 15th century painting: Perugino, Pinturicchio, Botticelli, Cosimo Rosselli, and Ghirlandaio. Michelangelo, commissioned by Julius II to decorate the **ceiling** (above and right), carried out the job — without any help — in only four years (1508-1512). The iconographic scheme is vast, starting with the *Creation* and continuing up to the *Redemption of Mankind*. Dozens of figures weave in and out of the architectural elements (both painted and real). These include: seven *Prophets* and five *Sibyls* (spandrels), twenty-two *forefathers of Christ* (lunettes above the windows), *saviours of the Hebrew People* (Esther, Judith, David), as well as several *nude figures* on the arcades bordering the Old Testament scenes whose meaning is, as yet, unknown. The subjects of the scenes in the nine rectangles in the center of the ceiling are: *Separation of Light from Darkness, Creation of the Universe, Separa-*

tion of Land from the Sea and Creation of the Animals, Creation of Adam, Creation of Eve, Fall of Man and Expulsion from Paradise, Noah's Sacrifice, the Flood and the Drunkenness of Noah. On the end wall is Michelangelo's dramatic **Last Judgment** (right) painted on a commission from Paul III, more than twenty years later (1536-1541). The complex composition involving 391 figures is wholly dominated by the stern figure of Christ the Judge, above which are angels and martyrs bearing symbols of their martyrdom and below which are angels with trumpets, with the elect going to heaven on the left and the damned being hauled off to hell on the right.

TIVOLI

Tivoli is situated on a hillside by the banks of the Aniene River. Among the Roman personages who sojourned in the splendid villas built as the patricians' country homes were Julius Caesar, Augustus, and Trajan. Hadrian's Villa, located in the environs, was the most celebrated in ancient Rome. Roman Tivoli was also renowned as the site of numerous temples, although little remains even of the largest which was consecrated to Hercules.

HADRIAN'S VILLA

The villa commissioned by Hadrian, among the most cultured of the Roman emperors, was built between 118 and 134 A.D. Of note are the *Pecile*, an immense quadriporticus (232 × 97 meters) around a pool and the *Island Nympheum*, encircled by a portico of Ionic columns and a kind of moat. The tiny villa which once stood on the island (today a heap of ruins) is believed to have been Hadrian's personal residence. The most interesting remains of the maze-like *Imperial Palace* belong to the huge peristyle known as *Piazza d'Oro* and an elegant hall known as the *Sala dei Pilastri Dorici*. The **Canopus**, a pool in the middle of a natural valley, was named after the place near Alexandria in Egypt that inspired it (left).

VILLA D'ESTE

The villa was originally a monastery that Cardinal Ippolito I D'Este commissioned Pirro Ligorio to remodel as his personal residence. The project (1550), took the Neapolitan architect almost twenty years to complete. Roman school painters such as Zuccari, Agresti, and Muziano, to name the most prominent, were commissioned to paint the fresco decoration. The park, with its over five hundred fountains, is considered one of the finest examples of the so-called "*Italianate garden*" (left: the **Ovato Fountain**).

FLORENCE

INDEX

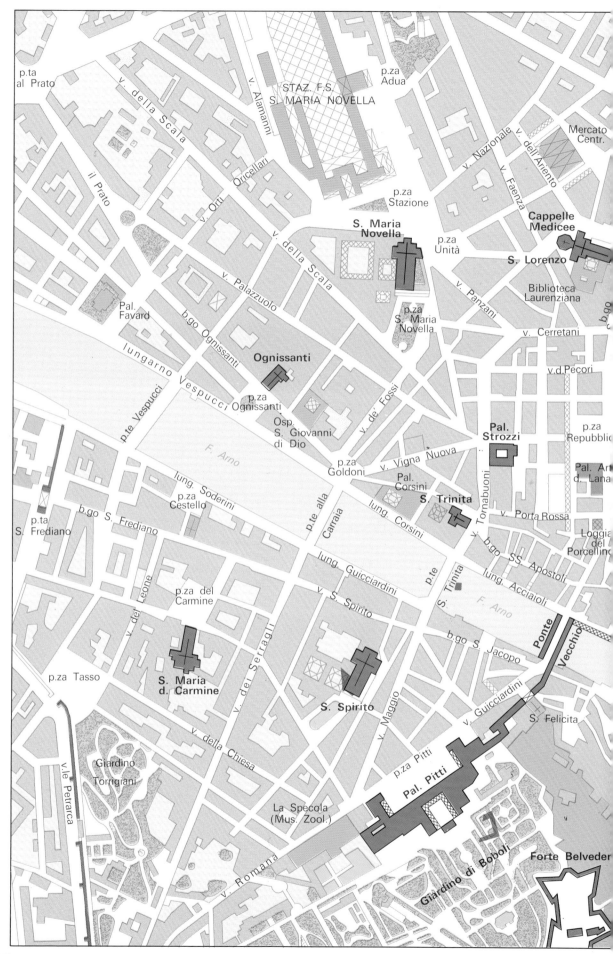

Cenacolo Apollonia

S. Marco

Museo di S. Marco

p.za S. Marco Ateneo

v. Guelfa

v. Battisti

SS. Annunziata

Giard. d. Gherardesca

Cimitero d. Inglesi

p.za Donatello

v. Cavour

v. Ricasoli

v. degli Alfani

Gall. d. Accademia

Museo Archeologico

v. Capponi

v. Giusti

Ginori

Pal. Medici-Riccardi

Spedale d. Innocenti

v. d. Colonna

S. M. Maddalena dei Pazzi

p.za D'Azeglio

v. Martelli

v. de' Servi

v. d. Pergola

borgo Pinti

v. Giusti

p.za

v. Bufalini

Ospedale S. M. Nuova

Farini

Tempio Israelitico

Battistero

p.za **Duomo**

Museo d. Opera d. Duomo

v. dell'Oriuolo

Teatro della Pergola

v. d. Pilastri

v. Carducci

p.za Giovanni

d. Duomo

v. S. Egidio

v. di Mezzo

S. Ambrogio

Calzaiuoli

v. d. Corso

v. d. Proconsolo

Pal. Nonfinito

b.go Albizi

v. Pietrapiana

b.go la Croce

v. Alighieri

Pandolfini

Badia

v. Ghibellina

v. dell'Agnolo

Allegri

p.za Ghiberti

rsanmichele

Bargello

p.za S. Firenze

Casa Buonarroti

v. Verdi

v. de' Pepi

v. Ghibellina

b.go

v. de' Macci

ggia della noria

p.za Signoria

Tribunale

b.go dei Greci

p.za S. Croce

v. S. Giuseppe

Pal. Vecchio

v. dei Neri

v. dei Benci

Magliabechi

S. Croce

v. Malcontenti

Uffizi

Castellani

p.za Mentana

lung. Diaz

c.so Tintori

Bibl. Nazionale

v. Tripoli

F. Arno

lung. d. Grazie

lung. Zecca Vecchia

lung. Torrigiani

p.te alle Grazie

F. Arno

costa S. Giorgio

v. de' Bardi

lung. Serristori

Museo Bardini

v. S. Niccolò

p.za Poggi

p.ta S. Niccolò

p.ta S. Miniato

Camping

v. di Belvedere

piazzale Michelangelo

FLORENCE "A NEW ATHENS"

Florence, dubbed "cradle of the Renaissance," "Athens of Italy," and just plain Firenze in Italian, was for over a thousand years a quiet town in the Tuscan countryside. Settled by the Etruscans, a Roman encampment, and a dominion of the Holy Roman Empire, its political and economic rise only began around the 11th-12th centuries when, despite warring between the Guelph and Ghibelline factions and recurrent revolts of the populace, prosperity from trade laid the way for its future position of leadership. In fact, by the 12th century, when it was a city-state and the first guilds (the famous *Corporazioni delle Arti*) were already functioning, the Florentine *fiorino* had become one of the strongest currencies in Europe. In the 13th century, the city's prosperity increased even more. This was the century dominated by Dante Alighieri, whose *Divina Commedia* written in the language spoken by the Florentines and not erudite Latin, laid the basis for modern Italian. In painting, Giotto and in architecture, Arnolfo di Cambio made their remarkable contributions. In the 14th century, a time of combined economic

hardship and plague (the Black Death of 1348 chronicled by Boccaccio in *Decameron*), Northern Gothic, known in painting as the International Style, was the strongest influence on the major Florentine artists, most of them followers of Giotto. In 1434, after the fall of the Communal form of government, Cosimo de' Medici, known as the Elder, seized power, an act which was to result in three centuries of Medici rule. By the second half of the century, the Renaissance (literally, rebirth) was well underway, as Cosimo's grandson, Lorenzo the Magnificent, presided over a remarkable court imbued with Classical-inspired Humanist culture. Under the patronage of the great Renaissance prince, the arts flourished to an extent that was to influence the cultural sphere all over the world, producing names such as Lorenzo himself, Poliziano, and Pulci in literature, Botticelli, the Lippis, Ghirlandaio, and Paolo Uccello, in painting, Brunelleschi, Michelozzo, and Alberti in architecture, and Donatello, Verrocchio, and the della Robbias in sculpture. Lorenzo was also a clever politician, managing to attain a correct balance of power

among the major contenders of his day, but his successors failed to live up to his greatness, with the result that the Medicis were driven from the city in the late 1400s and the citizenry proclaimed the Republic of Florence. Savonarola, Machiavelli, Michelangelo, and Leonardo were among the prominent figures who witnessed and took part in the events of those days. Shortly afterwards, however, the Medici triumphantly returned. Cosimo I, the first Medici grandduke, skillfully consolidated Florence's dominions in Tuscan territory, without relinquishing the great tradition of art patronage started by his predecessors. He was succeeded by Francesco I, another remarkable art lover who put together the first nucleus of the Uffizi collection. The Medici and their successors, the Lorraine grandukes, continued to promote artistic endeavors of every sort, although the political importance of Florence had, in the meantime, greatly declined. The outstanding events of the 19th century were the *Risorgimento* struggle and Florence's brief period as the capital of the newly-established Kingdom of Italy (1865-1871).

BAPTISTRY

Probably built around the 5th century, the Baptistry is a striking eight-sided green and white marble building (left). The sculpted doors on three sides are celebrated works: the **South door** with *Scenes from the life of St. John the Baptist* (below) by Andrea Pisano (1330), the *North door* with *Scenes from the New Testament* by Ghiberti (1401); the *East door* – one of the great masterpieces of Early Renaissance art – is the **Door of Paradise** (right) (as Michelangelo reputedly described it), sculpted with *Old Testament stories* by Ghiberti (1425-1452). The interior, is built on an octagonal plan and has two architectural orders. These consist of the lower part, which has granite columns with gilded capitals alternating with pillars, and the upper part, between whose smaller pillars are the windows of the so-called women's gallery where the women once sat during religious services, separated from the men. On the triumphal arch of the apse and on the cupola are splendid Byzantine style mosaics carried out by various Venetian and Florentine artists in the 13th and 14th centuries. The mosaics in the apse were begun in 1225 by Iacopo da Torrita. The apse is dominated by the huge figure of **Christ the Saviour in judgement** (below left).

GIOTTO'S BELLTOWER

Giotto started work on the huge green, pink and white belltower in 1334, although the project was completed after his death by Andrea Pisano and Francesco Talenti. The building is of remarkable grace and elegance. Some of the *reliefs* on the base of the building (copies, the originals are in the Museo del Duomo) while sculpted by Andrea Pisano are believed to have been designed by Giotto himself. The view from the 85-meter-tall tower is well worth the climb.

CATHEDRAL

When the old church of *Santa Reparata* (c. 4th-5th century) could no longer contain Florence's growing Christian community, Arnolfo di Cambio was commissioned to design a cathedral to be built right over it (1289). After his death in 1302, it was continued by artists of great renown such as Giotto, Andrea Pisano, and Brunelleschi (right). The **façade** (above), which was added in the 19th century, does not belong to the original project. Brunelleschi worked on the remarkable

dome from the 1420s to 1434. Of note are the cathedral's lateral portals: the early 15th century *Porta della Mandorla* (north side) and the 14th century *Porta dei Canonici* (south side). The feeling of stark majesty pervading the **interior** (above) is enhanced by the oversize pillars and impressive *stained glass windows* (14th-15th century). On the left wall are two celebrated frescoes commemorating 15th century military figures: **John Hawkwood** painted by Paolo Uccello in 1436 (further left) alongside the chiaroscuro **Niccolò da Tolentino** painted by Andrea del Castagno in 1456 (left). On the same side a little further on is a panel depicting *Dante and his Divine Comedy* by Domenico di Michelino (1465). A *Crucifix* by Benedetto da Maiano dated 1497 adorns the main altar. The dome is covered by the world's largest fresco, an impressive *Last Judgment* by Vasari, Zuccari, and helpers. A flight of stairs in the right aisle leads down to the *Crypt of Santa Reparata* which not only contains remains of the original Florentine cathedral, but also the recently-discovered tomb of Brunelleschi.

CATHEDRAL MUSEUM

The museum houses works originally part of the nearby religious complex. Its best-known treasure is Michelangelo's dramatic **Pietà** (right). Left unfinished, the group was sculpted around 1550 for the master's own tomb. This is perhaps the most dramatic of Michelangelo's four versions of the Pietà. Christ's lifeless body sinks down at the centre of the pyramid formed by the three figures supporting it: the Magdalen, on the left, with an expression of calm sorrow given her by Tiberio Calcagni, the pupil who finished the work after the master's death; the sorrowing Nicodemus, whose face according to Giorgio Vasari is a self-portrait of Michelangelo; Mary, her expressive power enhanced by the fact that she is rough-hewn in Michelangelo's characteristic "unfinished" manner. Other highlights include sculpture by Arnolfo, Donatello, and Nanni di Banco (from the original Cathedral façade), the two Cathedral *Cantorie* (Choir-balconies) — one by Luca della Robbia in 1438 and one by Donatello in 1455 —, Donatello's wooden *Mary Magdalene* carved in 1455 for the Baptistry, Andrea Pisano's **reliefs** for the Belltower (one detail above) as well as reliquaries, vestments, and a fine *altar frontal*.

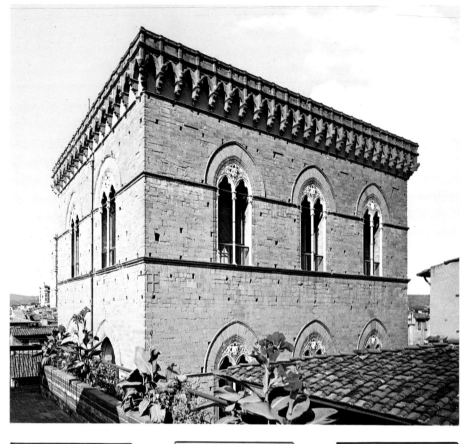

ORSANMICHELE

This imposingly massive building was designed by Arnolfo di Cambio in 1290 as a grain-market, with great storage chambers above, and was sited in the garden (orto) of the monastery of San Michele — hence the name. Burnt down in 1304 and rebuilt between 1337 and 1404 by Francesco Talenti and Neri di Fioravante in ornate Gothic style with elegant mullioned windows and archways, it was transformed into a church. The niches on the pillars outside contain the statues of the *Patron Saints of the Guilds* (14th and 15th cents.) by Ghiberti (*St. Matthew and the Baptist*), Nanni di Banco (*Four Crowned Saints*), Donatello (*St. George*) and Verrocchio (*St. Thomas*). The interior contains the Gothic *Shrine of the Madonna* by Andrea Orcagna (1359), with Bernardo Daddi's panel of the *Madonna and Child with a Goldfinch*, which was made in thanksgiving after the 1348 plague came to an end. On the 26th of July, each year, the banners of the guilds are hung around the church to commemorate the expulsion of the Duke of Athens from Florence (26 July 1343). Left, **Badges of the Major Arts or Guilds**. A fly-over bridge, built by order of Cosimo Ist, links Orsanmichele to the **Wool-merchants Guildhall** (14th cent, below). The shrine on the corner, contains a beautiful painting by Jacopo del Casentino.

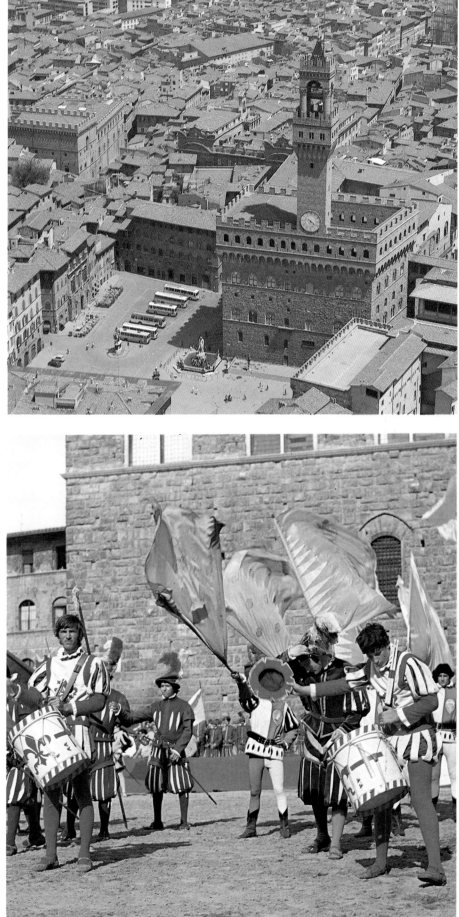

PIAZZA DELLA SIGNORIA

From the early 1300s when Palazzo Vecchio was being built to this day, the square has been the scene of all major Florentine political events. A plaque, for example, marks the spot where the reformer monk Savonarola was burned at the stake in 1498. Top right shows a **bird's eye view** of the square; bottom right, the Guards pay homage to the township during the **traditional football match** in period costume, which takes place on the 24th of June and is dedicated to St. John the Baptist, Patron of Florence. The south side of the square is dominated by the three great arches of the **Loggia della Signoria** which is also known as *Loggia dei Lanzi* because the Medici's Swiss

guards, the *Lanzichenecchi*, used to station under it in the 16th century and *Loggia dell'Orcagna* because it was once erroneously attributed to Orcagna (left). Designed in the 1380s by Benci di Cione and Simone Talenti for public ceremonies, it became an open air sculpture museum as great works such as Benvenuto Cellini's **Perseus**, 1554 (below left page 73) and Giambologna's **Rape of the Sabine Women**, 1583 (below) were placed under it; *Menelaos carrying the dead Patroclus*, a Roman copy of a Greek original, restored by Tacca; *Hercules slaying the Centaur Nessus*, a large and interesting group by Giambologna, which was finally placed in the Loggia after being displayed in various other places, in

1842. The **Fountain**, to the left of Palazzo Vecchio, is by Ammannati (below left, opposite), with the great statue of *Neptune* (popularly called Biancone - big whitey), surrounded by *nereids*, *tritons* and *sea-horses* (1575); left of the fountain is the *Equestrian Statue of Cosimo Ist de' Medici*, by Giambologna (1594). A copy of Michelangelo's **David** (below center) stands to the left of the main door of the Palace (the original being at the Galleria dell'Accademia), while Baccio Bandinelli's **Hercules and Cacus** stands on the right (below right). At No. 5 on the Piazza della Signoria, is the **Raccolta Alberto della Ragione,** a small, but interesting modern art collection (Campigli, Rosai, De Chirico, etc.).

PALAZZO VECCHIO

Arnolfo designed the building in 1299 and its **tower** in 1310, although modifications were made in the 14th-15th centuries and in the 16th by Vasari and Buontalenti (preceding page, above). The distinctive crenelated building with its rusticated stone facing and asymmetrical tower was a symbol of the Free Commune of Florence whose headquarters it was during the Middle Ages, even when it was later occupied by the powerful family of the Medicis, who governed the city and Tuscany from it. From 1865 to 1872 the Italian Chamber of Deputies, it is now Florence's city hall. The emblems below the crenelation represent the various ruling parties or families who governed Florence, while atop the 16th century portal is the symbol of Christ the king. The rampant lion grasping a lily, at the top of the tower simbolizes the liberty and the strength of the Republic of Florence. The main **courtyard** (above) designed by Michelozzo (15th century) was frescoed and stuccoed by Vasari (16th century). The **putto** (right) adorning the *fountain* is a copy of Verrocchio's 1476 original. The immense **Salone dei Cinquecento** or Hall of the 500 (opposite above), designed by Cronaca in

1495, was decorated by Vasari around the mid-1500s. Michelangelo's statue of *Victory* (1534) is in the centre of the west wall. Off the hall is the **Studiolo** (above) of Francesco I. Designed by Vasari and the Humanist scholar Borghini in 1572 for Francesco's collections, it was decorated by the foremost Mannerist artists of the 16th century. On the same floor, are the *Quartiere del Mezzanino* by Michelozzo, now a small art museum, the ***Loeser Collection***, featuring 14th-16th century Tuscan painting and sculpture) and the

Sala dei Duecento (Hall of the 200) designed by the Maianos. On the third floor are the Medici apartments: the **Quartiere di Eleonora di Toledo** (Cosimo I's wife) designed by Vasari, with a delightful *chapel* decorated by Bronzino (below right); the *Quartiere degli Elementi*, again by Vasari; the striking **Sala dei Gigli** (bottom right photo on page 75) with a carved portal by Benedetto da Maiano, frescoes (including one by Ghirlandaio dated 1485), and a coffered ceiling by Giuliano da Maiano. The *Cancelleria*

which contains a **bust of Machiavelli** who had his office here in the 15th century (bottom left photo on page 75). The **Wardrobe Room** (top right) was designed to house part of the treasures of the Medici family and later ot their successors, the Lorraines in the cupboards along its walls.

UFFIZI GALLERY

The building was commissioned in the 1560s by Cosimo I as offices (*uffizi*) from which to administer the affairs of state of his domain, the Granduchy of Tuscany. Vasari, the architect picked by Cosimo, came up with a design consisting of two **porticoed wings** joined by a shorter **arched portico** running parallel to the river (above and right). A few years later he completed a second project, this one in record time: the Corridoio Vasariano which runs from the Uffizi, crosses the river, and ends half a kilometer away at Palazzo Pitti. The Uffizi was turned into an art gallery by Bernardo Buontalenti in 1582 who received the commission from Cosimo's successor Francesco I. Buontalenti not only reorganized the rooms, but also added some new elements, e.g., the striking Tribuna. The collection, enriched over the years by Francesco's successors, became property of the state in 1743 when the last

of the Medicis, Anna Maria Ludovica, left it to the City of Florence. As space does not allow listing of all the masterpieces in the museum, only the most famous will be mentioned: three altarpieces representing the **Virgin Enthroned** (*Maestà*) by Cimabue (top right page 79), Giotto (top left page 79), and Duccio; **Annunciation** (left), by Simone Martini; *Adoration of the Magi*, by Gentile da Fabriano; **polyptych** from the church of the Badia by Giotto (bottom page 79), *Portraits of Battista Sforza* and *Federico da Montefeltro*, by Piero della Francesca; *Virgin and St. Anne*, by Masaccio and Masolino; *Battle of San Romano*, by Paolo Uccello; **Virgin and Child** (top right page 80), by Filippo Lippi; **Birth of Venus** (center left page 80), *Spring*, *Calumny*, and *Madonna of the Pomegranate*, by Botticelli. In the **Allegory of Spring** (top left page 80), painted in 1477 for Lorenzo di Pierfrancesco dei Medici, there are echoes of the verses of Polizano and of the ideals of the classical world which he had assimilated; *Portinari Altarpiece*, by

Hugo van der Goes; **Annunciation** (opposite page, above) and *Adoration of the Magi*, by Leonardo da Vinci; **Tondo Doni** by Michelangelo (opposite page, bottom right); *Virgin of the Goldfinch* and *Portrait of Leo X*, by Raphael; *Venus of Urbino*, by Titian; and *Bacchus*, by Caravaggio. Other renowned painters represented include Pontormo, Giorgione, and Canaletto and, among the non-Italians, Rubens, Van Dyck, Dürer, and Goya. Lastly, the *Corridoio Vasariano* is hung with self-portraits of Italian and foreign masters ranging from the 13th-14th century to the 20th. The "**Tribune**" of the Uffizi (left below) was built on an octagonal plan by Buontalenti (1585-89) in order to create a setting for the gallery's most precious and greatly admired works. The cupola was decorated with mother-of-pearl shell by Poccetti. Among the various marble groups exhibited here, the most outstanding is the **Medici Venus** (opposite page, bottom left), discovered during excavations of Hadrian's Villa at Tivoli, near Rome, and brought to Florence during the reign of Grand-duke Cosimo III. The 17th century *octogonal drawing table*, with its intricate design by Ligozzi and Poccetti, is one of the finest examples of Florentine semi-precious stone inlaid mosaic.

PONTE VECCHIO

The bridge is called Ponte Vecchio ("Old Bridge") because it is the oldest bridge in Florence; indeed there was a bridge here as far back as the time of the Etruscans. There is record of a wooden bridge here in 972; later destroyed and rebuilt in stone, it was destroyed once more by the savage flood in 1333. The present structure is that of Neri di Fioravante, who rebuilt the bridge, once again in stone, in 1345. The picturesque little shops which line it were once occupied by butchers, but in the 16th century by order of Cosimo I they were assigned to the silversmiths and goldsmiths who still sell their wares here. Above the shops on the left-hand side runs the famous corridor built by Vasari to link the Uffizi Gallery on one side of the river with the Palazzo Pitti on the other. The traces of the disastrous 1966 flood can still be detected on the buildings running along the left bank of the Arno. Left, a glimpse through the window of the Vasari corridor. The **bust of Benvenuto Cellini** in the center of the bridge stands against the background of Ammannati's *Santa Trinita bridge*.

PITTI PALACE

This remarkable palace was designed by Brunelleschi around the mid-1400s for Luca Pitti, a rich Florentine merchant. The original width of the building only included the seven central windows and was decorated on each of the three levels with roughly hewn rusticated blocks of sandstone. The Medici family bought the palace, enlarging it and altering it and moving into it in 1550 (above: **façade** - below: Ammannati's **courtyard**). The Medici also had the **Gardens of Boboli** laid out to designs by Tribolo (page 84, above). Further transformations occurred in the 17th and 18th cents. Palazzo Pitti houses exceptionally important art collections: the **Palatine Gallery,** a series of halls and rooms beautifully frescoed by Ciro Ferri and Pietro da Cortona, where an inestimable collection of works of art are displayed in the 17th cent. manner; the **Monumental Apartments,** the **Modern Art Gallery** with its fascinating nucleus of works by the 19th Cent. Tuscan Macchiaioli and the **Silver Museum** housing goldsmiths' masterpieces, glass and gems. The **Throne Room** in the Monumental

Apartments (left). Right: an overall view of the **Saturn Room** with Ciro Ferri's frescoes. The works displayed in the Palatine Gallery include: the *Beauty*, the *Magdalen* and *Portrait of a Gentleman*, by Titian; **Return from the Fields** (below left, page 87), by P.P. Rubens; the **Veiled Woman** (above right page 87), by Raphael, where yielding feminine beauty is highlighted by gleaming grey silk trimmed with old gold. Her secret smile and the gentle grace of her hands remind one vaguely of Leonardo's Monna Lisa; the **Madonna of the Grand-duke** (page 87, below right) and the **Madonna of the Chair** (page 86, above), also by Raphael – this famous round panel was painted when he was at the height of his pictorial potential, around 1516. His model for the Madonna was Margherita Luti, a woman of the people, called the Fornarina (or baker's daughter). Constantly alive to the world surrounding him, Raphael drew ably upon the experience amassed by the group of artists at work at the papal court, harmonising the monumental plasticity of Michelangelo with the warm tones of Sebastiano del Piombo, using his vision to express a concept of beauty based on harmony of proportions and complete absence of passion. Worldwide admiration and popularity are the tribute paid to the deeply human and maternal feeling, the brilliant colours, the golden flesh tints, and the Latin

beauty of the faces. The *Madonna of the Impannata* (the cloth-draped window), the *Pregnant Woman* and a number of *portraits* by Raphael, including those of *Tommaso Inghirami*, **Agnolo Doni** (opposite, centre right) and *Maddalena Strozzi Doni*; *portraits* by Van Dyck, Velazquez, Sustermans; paintings by Perugino (the mysterious *Magdalen*), Veronese, Botticelli (the *Fair Simonetta*, Filippo Lippi (the ethereal *Madonna and Child*), Tintoretto,

Murillo, Salvator Rosa (a lovely series of imaginary *landscapes*), Flemish and Dutch painters (Van Poelenburg, Ruysch, Schalken, Jan Breughel the Elder). Below left: Volterrano's **Parish Priest Arlotto's Pranks**, opposite, above left: the **Venus Room** with Canova's *Venus Italica* in the centre, commissioned by Luisa Bacciotti, Napoleon's sister, to replace the Medici Venus in the "Tribune" of the Uffizi which had been taken to Paris.

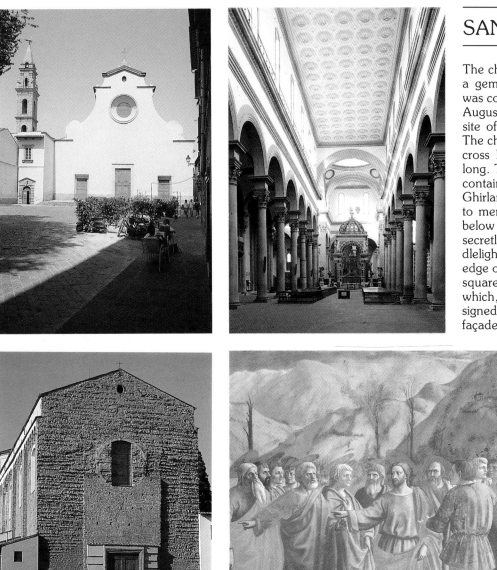

SANTO SPIRITO

The church designed by Brunelleschi is a gem of Renaissance architecture. It was commissioned by the monks of the Augustinian order and begun on the site of an earlier 13th century church. The church built in the shape of a Latin cross has three aisles and is 315 feet long. The 28 chapels running its length contain masterpieces by Donatello, Ghirlandaio, Lippi, and A. Sansovino, to mention a few. Here, in the cellars below the church, young Michelangelo secretly dissected corpses by candlelight so he could improve his knowledge of anatomy. On the far side of the square stands *Palazzo Guadagni* which, according to tradition, was designed by Cronaca about 1450. The façade is surmonted by a nice loggia.

SANTA MARIA DEL CARMINE

The original church dating from the second half of the 13th century was built for the Carmelite order. Decorated by Giotto, Taddeo Gaddi, Masolino, and Masaccio, it was almost completely destroyed in a terrible fire in 1771. The present church was built by Giuseppe Ruggeri (above left). The *Corsini Chapel* contains lovely Baroque sculpture by Giovan Battista Foggini and a monument to St. Andrea Corsini. In the museum is a noteworthy collection of frescoes detached from their original walls including Allori's grandiose *Last*

Supper mural. The *Brancacci Chapel* at the south end, right, is the most famous of all. Its walls are covered with an extraordinary fresco cycle which was begun by Masolino in 1424-1425, continued by Masaccio (1426-1427), and completed in 1485 by Filippino Lippi. In the **Tribute Money** Masaccio's full genius comes forth (above right). The immobile figures of the Apostles encircling the Savior and the large, silent group draw attention to the central part, where Christ's gesture is immediately mirrored by St. Peter. The

statuesque figures and the grave dignity of their postures stand out as a belief in the nature and importance of man, a belief already visible in Giotto a century before and reaffirmed by Michelangelo a century later. Masaccio's inventive power brought new vigor to the art of painting. Botticelli, Leonardo, and Michelangelo and many others have stood in mute admiration before his work. Next to the church is the cloister of the old convent where panels by the florentine painter Guarnieri illustrate the fresco technique.

SANTA MARIA NOVELLA

Built by Domenican monks in the mid-1200s, the church has a remarkable **façade** begun in the 14th century and completed by Alberti in the 15th (upper section and portal). The geometrical patterns recall the Tuscan-style Romanesque of the 11th-12th centuries (e.g., San Miniato, Baptistry, etc.). The entrance to the remarkable *cloisters* is to the left of the façade. The first, the *Chiostro Verde* (c. 1350), contains 15th century frescoes and the restored frescoes by Paolo Uccello (1430) once in the *Refectory*, which one enters next. The most famous scenes are those of the *Flood* and *Sacrifice of Noah*. From the other side of the Chiostro Verde you enter the *Chiostro Grande*, then the *Chiostrino dei Morti*, and finally the *Cappellone degli Spagnoli*. The Cappellone, built in 1350 and

taken over by Eleonora da Toledo's Spanish entourage for their religious services in the 16th century, was superbly frescoed by Andrea di Bonaiuto (c. 1355) with scenes from the *History of the Domenican Order* and the *Life of St. Thomas Aquinas*. The Gothic **interior** of the church (top right) contains numerous masterpieces of Renaissance art: Masaccio's **Trinity** frescoed around 1427 (bottom right), a *Crucifix* by Giotto, frescoes by Nardo di Cione and an Orcagna altarpiece (*Cappella Strozzi*), a celebrated Brunelleschi *Crucifix* (first chapel to the left of the choir), stupendous *Scenes from the Lives of the Virgin and St. John the Baptist* frescoed by Domenico del Ghirlandaio in the late 15th century. Michelangelo, aged 13, was sent to learn the rudiments of mural painting

from Ghirlandaio while he was working on the great fresco cycle; what he learned would later prove an invaluable aid when he was faced with frescoing the Sixtine Chapel. The *Strozzi chapel* to the right of the choir was frescoed by Filippino Lippi (1497-1502) with *Episodes from the life of St. Philip*, patron saint of the Tanners' Guild.

PALAZZO MEDICI-RICCARDI

A superb example of 15th century Florentine civic architecture, the palace was designed by Michelozzo in the mid-1400s for Cosimo the Elder and later embellished under Lorenzo the Magnificent. Purchased by the Riccardi family in the 17th century, it underwent remodelling and enlargement. The first floor of the exterior is faced in rough stone, the second in rusticated stone and the top one in planed blocks. Two of the ground floor windows (the corner ones) are traditionally ascribed to Michelangelo. From the courtyard radiate the **Museo Mediceo** (temporary exhibitions) on the left, an attractive *garden* in the center, and the *Cappella* (stairs to the right). Built by Michelozzo, the chapel was frescoed in 1460 by Benozzo Gozzoli with a scene ostensibly showing the *Wise Men on their way to Bethlehem* (actually portraits of the Medicis). Upstairs in the *Gallery*, an impressive hall frescoed by Luca Giordano in 1683. Lorenzo the Magnificent, the great patron of arts and letters, was born here in 1449.

SAN LORENZO

The church was built after a design by Filippo Brunelleschi (1425) on the site of an earlier basilica that had been destroyed in a fire. It is one of the most outstandingly fine examples of Early Renaissance religious architecture in Florence (right). Located right near the Medici Palace, it served as parish church for the Medicis who donated and commissioned numerous works of art for it. The nave of the harmonious grey stone interior is flanked by round arches which are supported by columns adorned with Corinthian capitals. Notable works are: two bronze *pulpits* by Donatello (1460s), Rosso Fiorentino's striking *Marriage of the Virgin*, a *tabernacle* by Desiderio da Settignano, and an *Annunciation* by Filippo Lippi. The *Tomb of Giovanni and Piero dei Medici* by Verrocchio (1472) is in the *Old Sacristy*, designed by Brunelleschi and decorated by Donatello. In the square in front of the church is a *statue of Giovanni dalle Bande Nere*, the only real military leader to have come from the ranks of the Medici family, by Baccio Bandinelli (1540).

MEDICI CHAPELS

There are two tomb complexes: the **Cappella dei Principi** (right), the grandduke's grandiose burial hall lavishly faced with coloured marble and semiprecious stones, and the *New Sacristy* designed by Michelangelo in 1524. Some of his most celebrated sculpture adorns the tombs: **Day** and **Night** above Giuliano of Nemours (right below), *Dawn* and *Dusk* above Lorenzo of Urbino, and the **Virgin and Child** (bottom left) above Giuliano and Lorenzo the Magnificent. Michelangelo's intent was to create a sense of solemn grandiosity by a carefully planned combination of architectural and sculptural elements. The square room with its imposing dome actually does give a feeling of movement as each architectural element emphasizes the plastic vitality of its forms. The message the chapel is supposed to convey is that the spherical perfection of eternity transcends human life constricted remorselessly by the passage of time symbolized by Michelangelo's allegorical figures representing Day, Night, Dawn, and Dusk above the two sarcophagi.

SANTISSIMA ANNUNZIATA

Built by Michelozzo between 1444 and 1481 on the site of a pre-existing 13th century oratory, the church was completed by Alberti who designed the dome. To the right of the church's portico is the Renaissance **Hospital of the Innocents** designed by Brunelleschi (left). The hospital was constructed as a refuge for orphans and abandoned children. The spaces between its nine harmonious arches are decorated with terra-cotta **tondoes** by Andrea della Robbia (below). The bronze **fountains** are by Tacca (bottom left).

ARCHAEOLOGICAL MUSEUM

The museum building is a 17th century palace, *Palazzo della Crocetta*, set in an attractive garden. The collections (established in the late 1800s) comprise Egyptian, Greco-Roman, and Etruscan art. In the ground floor halls are several noteworthy ceramics including the celebrated **François Vase** (left), a 6th century B.C. Greek black figure vase unearthed by a Frenchman, François, in an Etruscan tomb in Chiusi, as well as Attic and Etruscan copies of Greek vases, and Etruscan funerary urns (outstanding of which is the so called *Mater Matuta*). The highlights of the upstairs **Egyptian Collection** are a red basalt *pharaoh's bust* (18th century B.C.), and two painted *statues of servant girls engaged in household tasks*. The second section, the **Etrusco-Greco-Roman Antiquarium**, features masterpieces of Etruscan art (the *Chimera* and the *Haranguer*) and Greek sculpture (the *Little Idol* and a Hellenistic *horse's head* which inspired Donatello's horse for the Gattamelata monument in Padua), and Roman art.

MUSEUM OF ST. MARK'S

The museum building, the Monastery of San Marco, was built by Michelozzo between 1444 and 1481. Among the famous men who lived here were Fra Angelico, Savonarola, and fra Bartolomeo. The main courtyard, the *Chiostro di Sant'Antonino*, was frescoed by Angelico, as was the *Chapter Room*; opposite the entrance: *Crucifixion*. In the so-called *Ospizio del Pellegrino* (Pilgrims' Lodgings) is a collection of superb Fra Angelico panel paintings, including the celebrated *Linaioli Altarpiece* (1433), the *Bosco ai Frari Altarpiece*, the *St. Mark Altarpiece*, the remarkable *Last Judgment*, and smaller panels with *Scenes from the life of Christ*. The most striking in the room, however, is the *Deposition*, acclaimed as Fra Angelico's masterpiece (c. 1435). Upstairs are the austere monks' cells and the spiritually delicate *New Testament scenes* that Fra Angelico and his helpers, frescoed on the walls between 1439 and 1445. Fra Angelico's exquisite, almost calligraphic style is simplified, partly for technical reasons, in his frescoes. His precise details are reduced to a minimum, and clear pink and grey tones predominate. (See **Noli me tangere**, right and the **Annunciation**, below). Framed by the architecture of Michelozzo, the heralding angel and the Virgin are painted with great simplicity and clarity and a religious inspiration without precedent in history of art. Other outstanding frescoes by Fra Angelico are the *Coronation of the Virgin*, the *Flight into Egypt*, and the *Transfiguration*.

GALLERY OF THE ACADEMY

Established in 1784, the museum features 13th-16th century Florentine school paintings and some of Michelangelo's most famous sculptures. The main exhibition halls, the *Salone* and **Tribuna** (above) designed by Emilio De Fabris in the late 1800s, host Michelangelo's sculpture. Along the Tribuna are the four **Slaves** (left and top page 95), roughed out masterpieces of enormous vigour, meant for Pope Julius' (never finished) tomb in Rome (c. 1518), *St. Matthew* (c. 1505), the only one of the planned group of apostles ever carved for the Cathedral of Florence, and the **Palestrina Pietà** (center left page 95), a dramatic example of the master's late style. At the end of the Tribuna stands the **David** (right page 95), an early work of exceptional effect, that needs no introduction. It was commissioned by the Republic of Florence as the symbol of Florentine freedom and set right in front of Palazzo Vecchio, the city's civic center (where it stood until replacement by a copy became necessary for preservation in the 1800s). From a frontal position, the *David* seems almost relaxed, with the weight on the right leg, despite the splendid prominence given to the anatomical features and the dynamic tension visible in every part. In the right hand and arm, in the ribs and the abdomen, Michelangelo achieved a level of realism never seen before. In the face (one must move to the right-hand side of the stand to see it) there is a combination of pride and moral strength. The forehead and mouth express unyielding determination, and the eyes seem to burn with an inner fire. The *David* was created in the era of Amerigo Vespucci, Columbus, Machiavelli and Leonardo da Vinci. The statue thus represents more than just David, more than Apollo or even Hercules: in the end it is Michelangelo's monument glorifying the Renaissance man. Below, page 95 is the front of a 15th century **dower chest** showing the marriage of Boccaccio Adimari and Lisa Ricasoli. The rest of the museum focuses on Florentine painting, from the pre-Renaissance through Mannerist periods. Leaving the Academy, we find the *Conservatorio Musicale Luigi Cherubini*, to our left, at piazza Belle Arti 2.

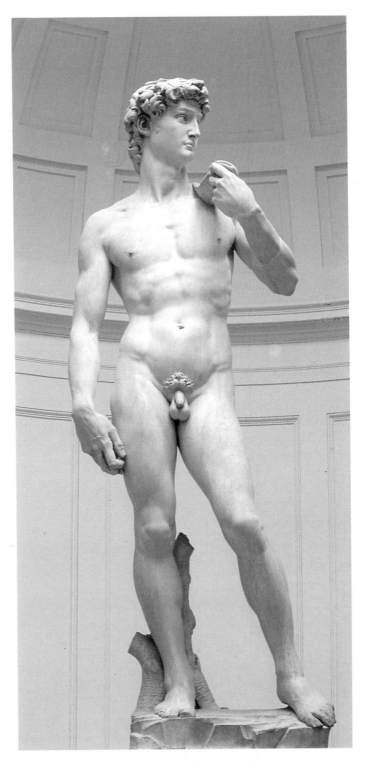

BARGELLO NATIONAL MUSEUM

The forbidding castle was built in 1225 as headquarters for the *Capitano del Popolo* (top left), a kind of governor. Thereafter, police headquarters (starting from the 16th century), it also served as a dungeon and was used for public executions. The bell in its crenelated tower is only rung on occasions of extraordinary importance (e.g., end of World War II and the flood of 1966). A museum since 1859, it vaunts one of the world's foremost collections of Tuscan sculpture. The *Museo Nazionale* starts in a *courtyard* filled with 16th century sculpture and emblems of various *podestà* (mayors) who governed the city. In the Salone del Cinquecento are famous 16th century masterpieces: Michelangelo's *Tondo Pitti*, **bust of Brutus** (left), *Drunken Bacchus*, and *Apollo David*, as well as sculpture by Cellini, Sansovino, Ammannati, and Giambologna. Upstairs is another collection of sculpture masterpieces, including Donatello's *St. George* (1416) and his celebrated **David** (bottom center page 97), as well as the reliefs of the **Sacrifice of Isaac** submitted by Ghiberti and Brunelleschi for the north door of the Baptistry (1402). Ghiberti's delicate rendering (above) won out over Brunelleschi's more dramatic version. The *Cappella del Podestà* was frescoed by a follower of Giotto. In the *Paradise scene* on the end wall is a celebrated *portrait of Dante*. On the third floor is a unique collection of Della Robbia **glazed terracottas** (top page 97). Bottom left page 97: the emaciated **St. John as a boy**, by Donatello: bottom right, page 97 the delightful **David** by Verrocchio.

SANTA CROCE

This magnificent Franciscan Gothic church was begun around the mid-1200s (according to tradition by Arnolfo di Cambio), although it was not consecrated until 1443. Italy's Westminster Abbey, it vaunts Giotto's remarkable frescoes, as well as the tombs of famous Italians. The **façade** is in 19th century Neo-Gothic style (right). In keeping with the Franciscan tradition, the interior (left) is simple and stately. The aisle walls, once covered with Giottesque frescoes, are lined with tombs and monuments including Vasari's **Tomb of Michelangelo** (left below), Canova's *Monument to Alfieri*, a *monument to Machiavelli*, as well as the *tombs of the composer Rossini, the poet Ugo Foscolo* (right aisle), *Galileo, and Ghiberti* (left aisle). The church is a veritable compendium of 15th century sculpture: Benedetto da Maiano *Pulpit*, Donatello's *Cavalcante* **Annunciation** (below), Rossellino's *Tomb of Leonardo Bruni* (right aisle) and Desiderio da Settignano's *Tomb of Carlo Marsuppini* (left aisle). Most of the chapels in the

righthand transept and side were frescoed in the 14th century (*Cappella Castellani* and *Cappella Baroncelli* by Gaddi, *Cappella Rinuccini* by Giovanni da Milano). Giotto's famous frescoes adorn two chapels of the east end, *Cappella Peruzzi* and *Cappella Bardi* (1317, *scenes from the life of St. Francis*). In the central **Cappella Maggiore** frescoed by Agnolo Gaddi is a wooden *Crucifix* by an unknown master (left). The last chapel on the left, the *Cappella Bardi di Vernio*, was frescoed by Maso di Banco (14th century). Nearby is a *Crucifix* by Donatello. The Museum of Santa Croce in the cloisters, shelters the **Crucifix** of Cimabue which was unfortunately tragically damaged by the 1966 flood, when the water rose to the height of over 5 metres (see picture on top). Below left: The **Madonna of the milk** by Rossellino. The Madonna was supposed to engender a plentiful flow of milk in feeding mothers.

PIAZZALE MICHELANGELO

With the whole city spread out below your feet, you see, from left to right; the Cascine Park, the dome and vast bulk of the Cathedral surrounded by the towers and belltowers of medieval Florence, Santa Croce, with the Arno in the foreground and the Florentine hills in the background. In the center of the square is a copy of the *David* commemorating Michelangelo.

SAN MINIATO AL MONTE

This superb Romanesque church was built between the 11th and 12th centuries. Inside, at the end of the nave is the *Cappella del Crocifisso*, designed by Michelozzo in 1448 and embellished with della Robbia terracottas.

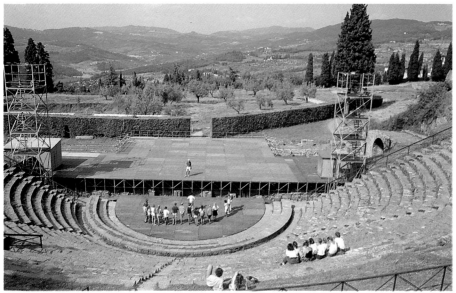

FIESOLE

This small Etruscan city, so old that its origins are lost in time, stands between two hills to the north of Florence. Its magnificent position, from which the entire valley of the Arno can be seen, its works of art and excavations revealing Etruscan and Roman ruins make it a compulsory stopping place for many visitors. The **Roman theatre** (left), discovered in 1809 during excavations of the ancient part of Fiesole undertaken in that year by the German baron Friedman von Schellersheim, goes back to the time of Silla (1st century B.C.), and was built in the manner of the Greek theatres. From the theatre there is a fine view of the hills.

VENICE

INDEX

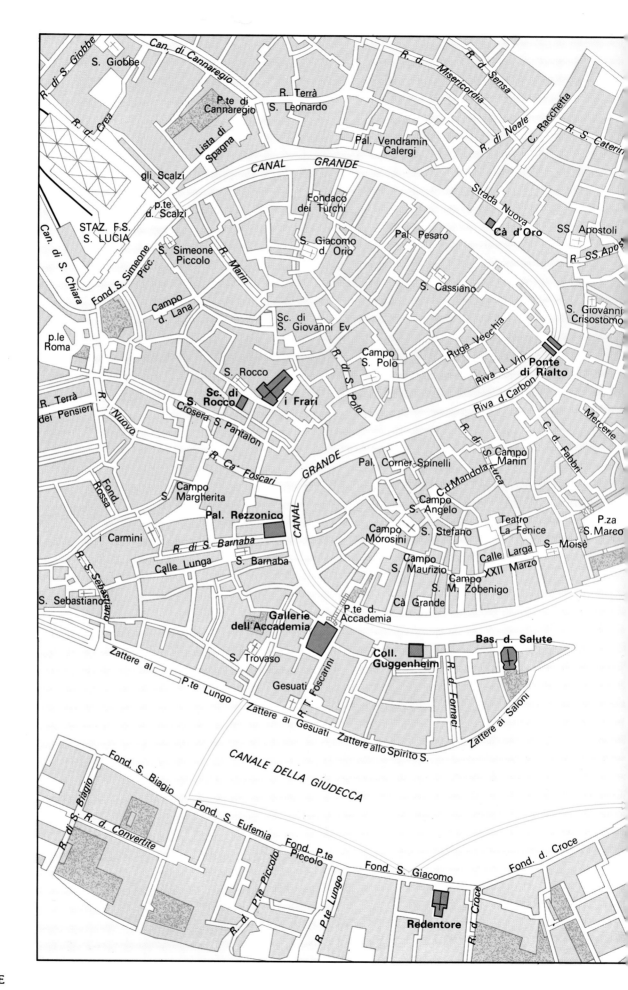

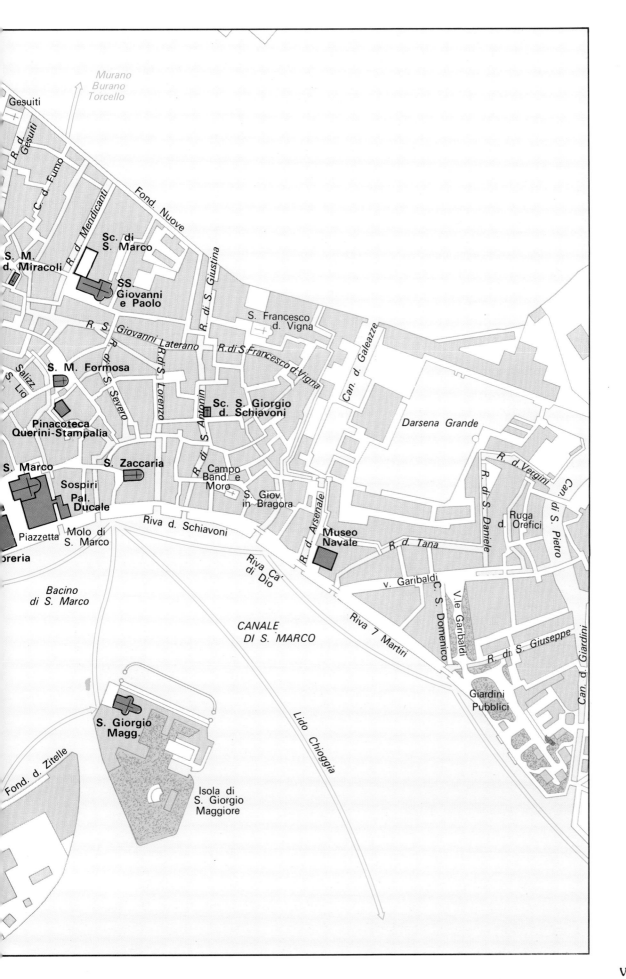

Gesuiti

Murano
Burano
Torcello

R. d. Gesuiti

C. d. Fumo

Fond. Nuove

R. d. Mendicanti

Sc. di
S. Marco

S. M.
d. Miracoli

SS.
Giovanni
e Paolo

R. di S. Giustina

S. Francesco
d. Vigna

R. S. Giovanni Laterano

R. di S. Lorenzo

R. di S. Francesco d. Vigna

Can. d. Galeazze

S. M. Formosa

S. Salizz.

S. Lio

R. di S. Severo

S. di S. Lorenzo

Sc. S. Giorgio
d. Schiavoni

R. di S. Antonin

Darsena Grande

Pinacoteca
Querini-Stampalia

R. d. Vergini

Can. di S. Pietro

S. Marco

S. Zaccaria

R. di S. Antonin

Campo
Band. e
Moro

R. di S. Daniele

Ruga
Orefici

Sospiri
Pal.
Ducale

S. Giov.
in Bragora

R. d. Arsenale

Museo
Navale

R. d. Tana

Piazzetta

Molo di
S. Marco

reria

Riva d. Schiavoni

v. Garibaldi

C. S. Domenico

V.le Garibaldi

Bacino
di S. Marco

Riva Ca'
di Dio

Riva 7 Martiri

R. di S. Giuseppe

Can. d. Giardini

CANALE
DI S. MARCO

Giardini
Pubblici

Lido Chioggia

S. Giorgio
Magg.

Fond. d. Zitelle

Isola di
S. Giorgio
Maggiore

VENICE "QUEEN OF THE ADRIATIC"

Venice is universally acclaimed as one of the world's most beautiful cities. It is certainly one of the most unusual. Actually, however, the buildings which appear so delicately suspended above the water are firmly earthbound, i.e., they are built on hundreds of islets and firmly reinforced by huge pylons sunk into the ground. The canals (*rii*) which separate the islands are the equivalent of mainland town streets — with the Grand Canal as Main Street. The area it stands on was a fishermen's village in the Roman era. Not until the Middle Ages, however, did it become a clearly defined political and social entity, when it came under the Byzantine sphere of influence, as opposed to the mainland cities which were dominated by the Longobards. In the 9th century, when most of Italy was under Frankish con-

trol, Venice embarked on a new form of government, i.e. a duchy headed by a duke (*Doge*, in Venetian dialect) and backed by the local nobility. Having severed all ties with the Empire of the East, she enjoyed long centuries of prosperity and glory: the *Serenissima* emerged as a leader in sea trade (especially with the Orient) and in culture. Her artistic development was totally unique. Her mixed Eastern-Western background made her a meeting place for two different cultural heritages. She never went through a feudal period, nor did she exist as a city-state. Rather, the Venetian form of government was that of an aristocratic republic. The great wealth amassed thanks to the business acumen of the Venetian traders (among them Marco Polo in the 13th century), was a prime factor in spark-

ing-off a great building boom. Venice reached the height of building up her political and economic power during the 15th and 16th centuries. She managed to extend her dominions on the mainland considerably and was successful in defeating the Turks in battle. At the same time, Venetian art was thoroughly revolutionizing Italian painting: the Bellinis, Carpaccio, Giorgione, Titian, Tintoretto, and Veronese were active during these years. Then, in the 17th and 18th centuries, as Venice found herself crushed by the new European powers, decline, both economic and political, began to set in. In 1797 she was annexed by Austria and did not regain her independence until 1866 when she joined the Kingdom of Italy. Thenceforth the history of Venice has merged with the history of Italy.

Arrival in Venice

Everyone who drives to Venice has to park in the **Piazzale Roma** (photo above). The Piazzale is connected to the mainland by the Ponte della Libertà built in 1933 alongside the railroad bridge completed in 1876. The building of the bridge and piazzale, which incidentally stirred a hornet's nest of controversy, was made necessary by the impelling need to facilitate both cargo and tourist connections with the mainland. Thus, Venice was able to avoid the isolation it would have necessarily faced had the structures required for its economic development and burgeoning tourist trade not been planned and carried out in time. If, on the other hand, you reach Venice by train, you get out at the **Santa Lucia Station** (top right). The station was named after the Palladian church originally on the site, which was torn down in the middle of the 19th century to make way for the railway line. Officiating at the inauguration (1846) of the bridge was General Radetzky representing the Emperor of Austria. Its construction was quite an engineering feat: 225 spans are supported by 75,000 pylons anchored in the muddy depths of the lagoon. On the other hand, the station is actually a recent construction (it was inaugurated in 1954). Leaving Piazzale Roma or the station as the case may be, we are now ready to enter the heart of the city by way of its main "thoroughfare", the **Grand Canal** (bottom right). The most widely used means of getting around in Venice is the vaporetto (a kind of water-bus).

GRAND CANAL

Venice's major waterway, the Grand Canal bisects the whole city. Running from the railway station to San Marco (approximately 1.50 kilometres as the crow flies), it is shaped like an upside down "S". Its vital statistics are: almost 4 kilometres long, maximum depth 5 meters, and average breadth 50 meters. Heavily trafficked by *vaporetti*, gondolas, and craft of every size and shape, the canal is a unique sight, its banks lined with an incredible parade of medieval palaces and churches. Where it starts (by the railroad station) is a Baroque building with a fine 17th century facade, the church of the *Scalzi*. The bridge crossing the canal here, **Ponte degli Scalzi** (left), was built in 1934. A bit further on the left, where the *Cannaregio Canal* intersects the Grand Canal, is *Palazzo Labia*. On the right is the **Fondaco dei Turchi** (below). The building was once the headquarters and trade center of the Orien-

tal merchants stationed in Venice. Once we have passed the *Rio della Maddalena*, we encounter on the left a whole series of picturesque buildings, e.g.: the 17th century *Palazzo Rouda* with its completely remodelled façade. Just beyond we note the 16th century *Palazzo Giussoni Grimani della Vida* attributed to Sanmicheli. Next we see the *Palazzetto da Lezze*, the 17th century *Palazzo Boldù* with its rusticated stone ground-floor, and lastly the *Palazzo Contarini-Pisani*, 17th century as well, with its spacious portico on the canal side. After the church of *San Stae*, is **Palazzo Pesaro** (below), a majestic building with a rusticated stone façade. Designed in the 17th century by Baldassarre Longhena, today it houses two important museums, the **Galleria d'Arte Moderna** and the **Oriental Museum**. A bit beyond on the left side is the renowned **Ca d'Oro** (right), with a stunning façade of Gothic marble tracery. It was designed by Bartolomeo Bon and Matteo de' Raverti in the 15th century. Inside is the **Galleria Franchetti** featuring works by Bellini, Tit-

ian, Carpaccio, and Guardi. Beyond the Rialto, on the left bank, are two Venetian-Byzantine style palaces, *Palazzo Loredan* (the Venice City Hall) and *Palazzo Farsetti*. A bit farther on the same side is *Palazzo Corner Spinelli* designed by Codussi in the 16th century. Just beyond the bend in the canal appears the striking façade of *Ca' Foscari*, an elegant 15th century Gothic design with three superimposed loggias. Just beyond, on the curve itself, is **Palazzo Rezzonico** (above) (***Museum of 18th Century Venice***). Opposite is an 18th century palace, *Palazzo Grassi*. Leaving the bend, you pass beneath the *Accademia Bridge*, a wooden structure first built in 1930 (now restored). The *Accademia Museum* is on your right. Beyond, on the left, is **Ca' Grande** or *Palazzo Corner* (left) built by Sansovino in 1537. The last buildings on the right bank are the church of *Santa Maria della Salute* and the *Customs Point* (Punta della Dogana), built in the 15th century, for the levying of duties on ships merchandise. On the left is *San Marco*. From the canal you can see the *Doges' Palace*.

RIALTO BRIDGE

The Rialto is the oldest of the three bridges spanning the canal. Originally made of wood, it collapsed in 1440 and was rebuilt, again of wood, but this time with the addition of several shops along it. It had a special mechanism which allowed the middle section to be moved whereby even the tallest masted ships could sail through. It was somewhat unstable, though, and thus in the 16th century it was decided to rebuild it. A competition was called, attracting the participation of such well-known architects as Michelangelo and Sansovino, who devoted years to the project. Antonio da Ponte, the winner, started work on the great undertaking which he completed in 1592. The Rialto is a single span bridge, 28 meters in length (this is the narrowest point of the Grand Canal) and has a maximum height of 7.5 meters at the center. The two ends rest upon 12,000 wooden pylons sunk into the muddy depths.

SANTA MARIA DELLA SALUTE

The senate of the *Repubblica di Venezia* decreed that it be built in 1630 in thanksgiving for the end of a plague epidemic. Longhena, who was awarded the commission, brillantly overcame numerous practical problems relating to soil subsidence by reinforcing the dome drum with the aesthetically-pleasing curlicews that make the building so distinctive and unusual. The church is based on an octagonal design, has two domes, and faces out on the Grand Canal. The spacious interior is circular and surrounded by columns. The side altars are adorned with paintings by Titian, Morlaiter, and Luca Giordano. The magnificent *main altar* standing in the choir was designed by Longhena himself, and decorated with statues of saints carved by various sculptors. Alongside it is a fine 16th century bronze *candlestick*, while behind it is a 15th century *Virgin and Child*. The most important works, however, are in the *Sacrestia Grande* (Large Sacristy): *St. Mark Enthroned*, by Titian; a 12th century mosaic *Virgin and Child*; *Wedding at Cana*, by Tintoretto; *Sacrifice of Isaac*, *David and Goliath*, and *Cain and Abel*, by Titian.

PIAZZETTA

Until the 16th century the Piazzetta, i.e., the square between the San Marco Quay and Piazza San Marco, was a marketplace for foodstuffs and the scene of public life (above). On top of the two columns standing in the middle are statues of *St. Todaro* (or Theodore, one of the first patron saints of Venice) and a *Lion of St. Mark*. To your left (back to the water) is the **Libreria Marciana**, or **Libreria Sansoviniana** designed in the mid-16th century by Jacopo Sansovino for the rare book collection bequeathed to the city by the 15th century Greek humanist scholar, Cardinal Bessarione (right). Today the building houses a library: the *Biblioteca Nazionale Marciana* and Venice's **Archeological Museum**. The Piazzetta was also the scene of public executions and between these columns both humble citizens and high ranking personages were put to death. The right side of the Piazzetta is closed-off by the Doges' Palace.

PIAZZA SAN MARCO

Originally, Piazza San Marco was a grass-covered open space traversed by a canal and bounded at each of its shorter ends by a church. Subsequent transformation and embellishments made it into one of the most beautiful squares in the world. Today it is bounded by buildings on all four sides (above). To the east is the Basilica and to the west, the *Napoleonic Wing* (early 19th century). The long buildings to the north and south are the *Procuratie*, which served as the living and working quarters of the Procurators of St. Mark (overseers of public works). The *Procuratie Vecchie* (Old Courts) on the north side were built between the late 1400s-early 1500s. The *Procuratie Nuove* (New Courts) to the south were begun by Scamozzi in the late 1500s, and completed by Longhena in 1640. Two other important features complete the square: its attractive geometric paving, which dates from the 18th century, and two towers: the **Belltower** (right) and the **Clock Tower** with its great bronze bell on which the famous "Moors" strike the hours (left). The *Museo Correr* occupies the upper floor of the *Procuratie Nuove*.

BASILICA OF ST. MARK'S

In 828 the mortal remains of St. Mark the Evangelist were brought to Venice from Alexandria in Egypt. On this occasion it was decided to built a church worthy of containing such a precious relic, and one befitting a burgeoning city anxious to show off its wealth and grandeur. Most of the grandiose basilica was built between the 11th and 15th centuries. The result is a harmonious blend of Byzantine gilding, Gothic gables, Romanesque round arches, and Islamic domes. Five great *portals*, separated by Romanesque columns and reliefs, dominate the two-story **façade**

(above). Although the portal lunettes are all adorned with *mosaics*, only the first one on the left, dated 1270, which shows how the Basilica looked in the 13th century, is original. The others were made in the Baroque period. Four of the five arches of the upper level also bear mosaic decoration (18th century). Their elaborate carved frames were sculpted by the Dalle Masegne family during the 14th and 15th centuries. On the terrace separating the two levels are the famous gilded bronze *Horses* (recently replaced by copies, as the originals have undergone extensive

restoration). The four horses, brought to Venice from Costantinople by Doge Enrico Dandolo in 1204, were cast in Greece, probably around the 4th century B.C. On the corner of the Basilica (Doges' Palace side) is another celebrated sculpture group, the so-called *Tetrarchs*. This fascinating porphyry carving has been classified as a 4th century B.C. Syrian work. From the **largest portal** (right), you enter the Basilica **atrium** where the ceiling is decorated with *mosaics* (page 120). The finest are undoubtedly the *scenes from the Genesis* (13th-14th centuries).

The **interior** is in the shape of a Greek cross (right), with three aisles to each arm of the cross, and *matronei* (women's galleries to running the length of the upper level. *Mosaics* cover the walls and the floor (subject: the **lives of Christ**, above, and *St. Mark*). The Byzantine style mosaics were made between the 12th-13th centuries by Venetian craftsmen, while those of the inside façade were designed by Tintoretto and others. Even older mosaics (predating the year 1000) are to be found between the apse windows. The great **Christ**

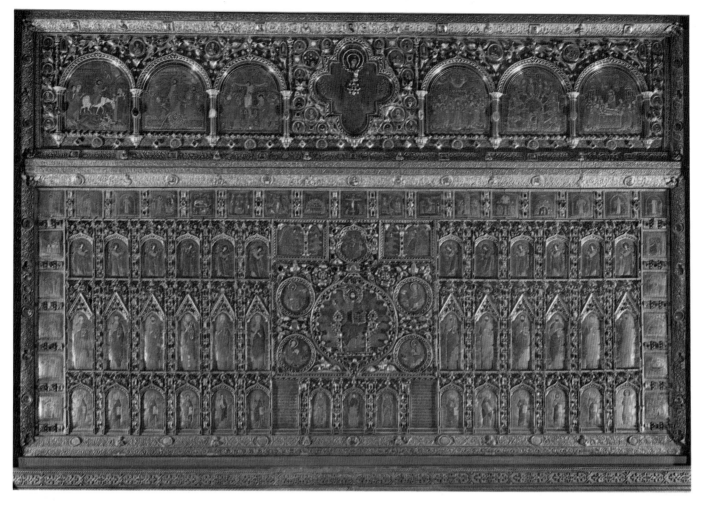

art, the **Pala d'Oro** (Golden Screen) (above and left). Made of gold, gemstones, and enamels, it was crafted between the 10th and 14th centuries. The enamel in the center depicts *Christ* with the *Evangelists*, while the *Virgin*, *Apostles*, and *Prophets* are portrayed in the others. On the right wall of the left transept is a famous Byzantine icon known as the *Madonna Nicopeia* (Victorious Virgin). Dated around the 10th century, it was brought to Venice from Constantinople by the returning crusaders in 1204. In the right aisle is the entrance to the **Baptistry** (right), which has kept its present form since 1350 when the Doge Andrea Dandolo commissioned it. In the center the large *Baptisimal Font*, designed by Sansovino, is adorned with marbles and mosaics (1545). The *mosaics* on the walls, vaults and domes, was carried out by Venetian masters of the 14th century. Returning to the Basilica atrium, go up one flight to the interesting *Museo Marciano* (or Museo dell'Opera di Palazzo) and the outdoor terrace where the Greek horses are displayed. Following pages: a fine wiew of the **Doges' Palace**.

(top left page 121) in the apse, however, dates from the 16th century. A carved screen separates the nave from the choir. The fourteen statues adorning it were sculpted in the 14th century by the Dalle Masegnes. On either side are pulpits: the 14th century *double pulpit* and the so-called "Reliquary Pulpit." The relics of St. Mark are preserved inside the richly-decorated *main altar*. Behind the altar is one of the masterpieces of medieval

DOGES' PALACE

The stunning combination of delicate Gothic tracery, pointed arches, and patterned stonework makes the building appear light and airy, almost as if it were weightless. The palace was built in the 9th century as the doges' residence, and then altered several times by famous architects such as the Dalle Masegnes, Rizzo, and da Ponte. The majestic *balcony* on the lagoon side was sculpted by the Dalle Masegnes in 1404, whereas the one facing into the Piazzetta, carved by followers of Sansovino, dates from 1536. The elaborate portal you pass beneath to enter the building, the *Porta della Carta* (Door of the Bills), was carved by members of the Bon family in 1442. In the **courtyard** are two 16th century *bronze wells* (above). On the left is the so-called *Foscari Arcade*. The monumental staircase of the adjoining *Cortiletto dei Senatori*, the **Scala dei Giganti** (Giants' Staircase), was designed by Rizzo in

the 1500s (left below). It has been given this name because of the enormous statues of Mars and Neptune sculpted by Sansovino. At the top of these stairs the Doge was crowned as soon as he was elected, in the presence of the people and the dignitaries of the Republic. Ambassadors and illustrious guests were also received here. A series of decorated halls, most of them the work of the great 16th century Venetian masters, starts on the second floor. We shall list only the highlights. In the *Sale della Pinacoteca* (Picture Gallery rooms), once the doges' private apartments: **Lion of St. Mark** (top page 106), by Carpaccio, *Pietà* by Giovanni Bellini, and works by Hieronymus Bosch; in the **Sala delle Quattro Porte** (Room of the Four Doors) (above): frescoes by Tintoretto and a Titian painting depicting **Doge Antonio Grimani kneeling before Faith** (right); in the *Sala del Collegio* (Room of the College): a superb ceiling adorned with paintings by Veronese; in the *Sala del Senato* (Senate Room): paintings by Tintoretto (on the ceiling, *Venice*,

Queen of the Seas); in the Sala del Consiglio dei Dieci (Room of the Council of Ten) (left above): paintings by Veronese. Here, the highly feared magistrates assembled to investigate crimes of a political nature against the security of the State. In the **Sala della the Bussola** (Room of the Booth) paintings by Veronese and Aliense (below left). In the foreground the double door called the "Bussola" after which the room is named. It was here that the condemned and accused waited for decisions on their crimes against the security of the Republic. In the **Sala d'Armi** (Armoury) are exhibited arms and armour of great renown (top). This collection of 15th and 16th century pieces is truly unique, as it is made up of weapons really used to defend the palace (plus parade and jousting arms). By 1317 the Doge's Palace already had its own armoury, but then in 1532 this room was selected as the new arsenal. Although numerous pieces were dispersed, especially during the French looting of 1797, the collection presently totals about 2000 objects. To the right, the **bust of Francesco Morosini**, a heroic Venetian admiral. In the **Sala del Maggior Consiglio** (Hall of the

Greater Council) the supreme Venetian magistrates gathered in council. The room measures 176 feet long, 82 feet wide, and 51 feet high (above). Destroyed by fire in 1557, it was rebuilt by Antonio da Ponte and embellished with paintings whose iconography involve the glorification of the Venetian Republic. Upon entering you are immediately struck by the huge painting above the tribune. It represents *Paradise* and was painted by Tintoretto. A large oval panel on the ceiling, by Paolo Veronese, depicts the **Apotheosis of Venice**, with splendid perspective and scenic effects (right). To the left, the **Sala dello Scrutinio** (Voting Room) rebuilt by Antonio da Ponte after the fire of 1577. The paintings which celebrate the victories of the Venetian Republic on the high seas were suggested by Girolamo de' Bardi. The Triumphal Arch against the far wall was built by A. Tirali in 1694 to honor Doge Francesco Morosini. On the righthand wall are the *Battle of Lepanto* by A. Vicentino and the *Victory of the Dardanelles* by Liberi.

BRIDGE OF SIGHS

The bridge with its graceful pink outline standing out against the shadowy recesses of the canal, joins the Doges' Palace to the 16th century Prigioni Nuove (New Prisons) and was designed by Antonio Contini in the decorative 17th century Baroque style. The sighs the bridge was named for actually go back to a 19th century Romantic tradition; they had nothing to do with sighs of love, but were probably the much more tragic exhalations of the condemned as their last glances at Venice pierced the grille windows along the way. Left, a **cell** in the *pozzi* (dungeons). Beyond the Ponte della Paglia we continue down the *Riva degli Schiavoni* now a favorite promenade and once the mooring station for trading vessels coming from Dalmatia and other Slavonic ports.

ISLAND OF ST. GEORGE

Looking ahead, from the harbor of St. Mark's, we cannot help noticing the Isle of St. George (top and right), with the lovely white façade of the **Church of San Giorgio Maggiore** standing out against the red brick buildings. The façade designed by Palladio in 1565 (together with the church) repeats one of the great architect's favorite motifs, the so-called "giant order", i.e. four enormous Corinthian columns supporting a huge triangular tympanum surmounted by statues. The plain, but highly elegant, cruciform interior contains some outstanding Tintorettos such as the *Last Supper* and *Shower of Manna*. The adjoining monastery is now occupied by an art and cultural organization, the Cini Foundation — thanks to which the whole architectural complex was restored.

ACADEMY GALLERIES

The *Accademia di Pittori e Scultori* was founded in 1750. Piazzetta, its first director, was succeeded by Tiepolo in 1756. In the late 1700s it was moved to its present location on the Grand Canal inside a former monastery, the Convento della Carità. Many prominent artists, including Canova, trained here, althogh gradually the Accademia became more of a museum than an art school. The plural "*Gallerie*," as the museum is called in Italian, is used because originally there were two separate collections, one of plaster casts and one of paintings. Today, it ranks as one of the world's great art museums. The first exhibition hall is primarily devoted to the 14th century Venetian school. Major works include: *Coronation of the Virgin*, by Paolo Veneziano; *Mystic Marriage of St. Catherine* and *Annunciation Altarpiece*, by Lorenzo Veneziano; *Madonna della Misericordia* and *Coronation of the Virgin*, by Jacobello del Fiore. Top: Antonio Vivarini's robust 15th cent. **Madonna and Child**. Room II: *Madonna and Saints* and *Virgin of the*

Orange Tree by Cima da Conegliano; the *Calling of the Sons of Zebedee* by Marco Basaiti. Room III: *Madonna and Saints*, attributed to Sebastiano del Piombo. Room IV: **St. George** (left), by Mantegna and *St. Jerome and donor*, by Piero della Francesca. Room V: *Pietà, Madonna degli Alberelli*, and *Al-* *legories*, all by Giovanni Bellini, and Giorgione's masterpiece, the unsettling **Tempest** (above). Room VI: works by Tintoretto and Titian. Room VII: **Portrait of a Gentleman**, by Lotto (below left, following page). Room VIII: works by Palma the Elder. Room X: *Banquet in the House of Levi*, a huge canvas by Paolo Veronese, and the *Miracles of St. Mark* cycle, by Tintoretto. Rooms XI through XV are devoted to Tintoretto, Veronese, 16th century Venetian school, Tiepolo, and 18th century landscapists. Room XVI: four mythological scenes by Tiepolo. Room XVII: **landscapes** by Guardi (bottom page 106),

Bellotto, and Canaletto, pastels by Carriera, and genre scenes by Pietro Longhi including the *Fortune-Teller*, the *Dancing Lesson*, and the *Pharmacist*. Room XVIII: sculpture by Canova. Room XX: the renowned series of 15th century Bellinis and Carpaccios depicting the *Miracles of the Reliquary*, and especially: **Healing of a Possessed Man**, by Carpaccio (page 107), and **Procession in Piazza San Marco** (top), by Gentile Bellini. Room XXI: Carpaccio's remarkable cycle of the *Story of St. Ursula*. The photos on page 137 show the **Arrival of the Ambassadors** (top), **St. Ursula meets Ereus** (bottom left) and the **Burial of St. Ursula** (bottom right). The story of Ursula, the virgin princess from Brittany, martyred during the Huns' siege of Cologne, is narrated in Carpaccio's inimitable style, combining fanciful flights of imagination to careful observation of down-to-earth everyday detail. The following hall is devoted to the 15th century, while the last room, with a remarkable gilded carved ceiling, contains outstanding works by Titian (*Presentation of the Virgin*) and Giovanni Bellini.

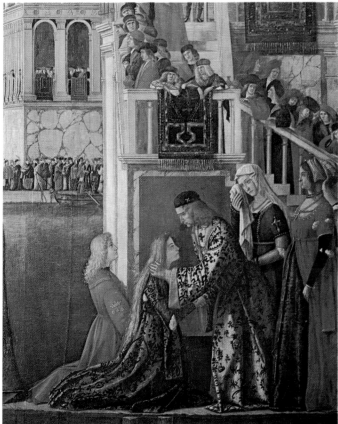

SAN GIOVANNI E SAN PAOLO

This huge church was begun in 1246 as part of a monastery. The **façade** with its portal by Bartolomeo Bon was left unfinished in the mid-1400s (left). The area in and around the apse is especially noteworthy. The fact that there is no belltower is quite unusual. Several historical Venetian figures are buried in the church. The most important are: *Admiral Marcantonio Bragadin* (right aisle, 16th century tomb) and *Doge Pietro Mocenigo* (inner façade, 15th century tomb by Pietro Lombardo). Among the other notable works adorning the building are: the *St. Vincenzo Ferreri Altarpiece*, by Giovanni Bellini (second righthand altar); *St. Antonino giving alms*, by Lorenzo Lotto (right transept); and a splendid chapel, the *Cappella del Rosario*, with paintings by Veronese and a canvas attributed to Moretto. The statue in the square is Andrea del Verrocchio's 1496 masterpiece, the **Monument to Bartolomeo Colleoni** (*Condottiero* of the Republic of Venice). Begun in 1481, it was cast in the 1490s by Alessandro Leopardi, who was also responsible for its pedestal (below left).

SANTA MARIA GLORIOSA DEI FRARI

Also known as Santa Maria Assunta, the Church of the Friars on the Campo of Santa Maria Gloriosa dei Frari is one of Venice's most important monuments (right). Like San Zanipolo, its great rival as an artistic treasure house, it contains the tombs of several rich and famous Venetians. Begun by the Franciscan monks around 1520 — some claim after a design by Nicola Pisano, the great architect and sculptor active in Tuscany — it was reelaborated and enlarged by Scipione Bon in 1338 and not finished until 1443. The stark Romanesque-Gothic **façade** is divided into three sections which echo the three aisles inside the church. Above the portal is a statue of Christ Resurrected by Alessandro Vittoria, flanked by two figures attributed to the school

of the Bon family. The **interior** of the church of Santa Maria Gloriosa conveys an impression of great stateliness (above). Twelve round columns joined by tie rods divide the nave from the aisles. Above are simple brick ribbed ogival vaults that enhance the church's solemn spaciousness. The exquisite choir in the center contains fine sculptures by Bartolomeo Bon and Pietro Lombardo. Two of Titian's most famous paintings are hanging here: the *Assumption of the Virgin*, dated 1518, and the *Ca' Pesaro Altarpiece*, dated 1526. Other notable works include an altarpiece portraying *St. Ambrose and other saints*, by Alvise Vivarini and Marco Basaiti; and a triptych depicting the *Virgin Enthroned* by Giovanni Bellini in the Sacristy. Among the tomb monuments, two belong to great artists: *Titian's* in the nave, built in the 19th century above the spot where the master was supposedly buried and *Canova's*, in the left aisle, designed by the sculptor himself.

SAN ROCCO

Dominating the triangular-shaped Campo San Rocco, is the 16th century *Scuola di San Rocco* (School of St. Roch). Of all the Venetian *scuole*, it is by far the most important one — if only for the number and quality of its Tintorettos. The great artist was given the commission to decorate the so-called Sala dell'Albergaria after a competition in which Paolo Veronese, Zuccari, and other equally famous artists took part. The ceiling of the *Sala dell'Albergaria* (on the upper floor), recently restored and regilded, has the *St. Roch in glory*, which was Tintoretto's winning competition entry. The great artist was engaged on the project from 1563 to 1588, painting scenes of the Passion around a superb *Crucifixion* of notable dimensions. Returning to the rectangular *Salone Maggiore* (Great Hall), we find a self-portrait of the artist aged 66

by one of the doorways. On the ceiling are *21 Old Testament scenes*, also by Tintoretto. To the left of the altar is an *Annunciation* by Titian, while along the walls there are *Scenes from the life of Christ*. In the nearby Sala della Cancelleria (Chancery Room) the *Ecce Homo* has been attributed to Titian. Downstairs, we enter the grandiose ground floor room divided by two rows of Corinthian pillars, also decorated by Tintoretto. The **Church of San Rocco** (photo right), originally a Renaissance building, was rebuilt in the 18th century by Giovanni Scalfarotto, its façade ispired by the graceful front of the Scuola. Inside the single-aisled church are several works by Tintoretto: the *Annunciation* (to the right of the organ) *St. Roch before the Pope* (on the left), and *St. Roch in the desert* (first altar on the right). There are also several fine paintings portraying *Scenes from the life of St. Roch* along the choir walls. An urn by the main altar contains the relics of the Saint.

High water

Venice is built upon piles of Istrian pinewood anchored into the lagoon to reinforce the islets on which the buildings stand. The sea, which has always supported the city's economic and political well-being, has often represented danger as well. Sudden tides and sea-storms have time and again threatened the fragile city — nobody will ever forget the terrible *flood of November 1966* which at first made it seem as though the city would never survive. The phenomenon of high tides (called "*acqua alta*" or high water in Venetian) is such a common experience that the Venetian have come to accept them philosophically, without making too much fuss. The water seems to have a special fondness for Piazza San Marco and the Basilica, where it can get more than 1 1/2 feet deep so that, as you can tell from the photo above left, one sometimes sees gondolas on the square, or even beneath the arcades. In the photo, the improvised wooden gangway for pedestrian traffic is clearly visible in the background.

LIDO OF VENICE

An elongated island in the Venetian lagoon, the Lido is a popular summer resort. Bordered by a great stretch of sandy beach, it possesses excellent tourist facilities, including fine hotels, a *casino*, and restaurants. The Venice Film Festival is held here every year (left below).

MURANO

Around the 10th-11th centuries it became one of the major lagoon centers. The tradition of *glassblowing*, still the basis of the city's great renown, dates back to that period, although it received its greatest boost in the 13th century. Much of the city appears as it did in the 15th-16th centuries when its villas and gardens were favorite vacation spots with the Venetian aristocrats. The **Glass Museum** is on the Canale di San Donato. One of the best-known pieces of the museum is the loving *cup* crafted by the *Barovier* masters, remarkable proof of the heights reached

by the glassmakers, who not only drew upon their imagination and skill, but also put in painstaking hard work. Next to the museum is **Santi Maria e Donato**, (right) a Ravennate-style church with a 12th century apse covered with geometric patterns, and a square *bell-tower*. The highlights of the striking interior include frescoes and the floor *mosaics*. One of the musts in Murano is a walk along the charming *Angeli* and *Vetrai* canals. Inside the 15th century church of *San Pietro Martire* on Rio dei Vetrai are paintings by Tintoretto, Giovanni Bellini and Veronese.

TORCELLO

This tranquil little island, today partially uninhabited, was once a mighty urban center and Venice's major rival. It was founded in 452 by refugees from the mainland city of Altino and by the 7th century had become an important bishopric. Torcello's decline was a result of two factors: overpowering competition from Venice and malaria, which, in a way, was just as overpowering. The island, is unrivalled for atmosphere. One devotee was Ernest Hemingway who spent long periods living and working on Torcello. The Ravennate-style *Cathedral* was built between the 8th and 11th centuries, whereas its square *belltower* dates from the 9th century. Inside the church, the choir is separated from the nave and aisles by a carved *screen* with remarkable 15th century icons and a wooden *Crucifix*. The mosaic adorning the inside façade (*Last Judgement*, 12th century) and apse zone (*Virgin and Child*, 13th century) are among the great masterpieces of Byzantine art. Next to the Cathedral is a 10th-11th century polygonal building, the church of **Santa Fosca** (right). Rebuilt in the 11th century, it has a distinctive exterior with a porch sustained by marble columns and brick pillars, and an octagonal apse. The Greek cross interior is midway between a square and circular shape, as the plans to add on a dome were never carried out. Outside, opposite Santa Fosca, is the so-called *Caregon* (chair, in the local dialect), which was once called "Attila's Throne", although it was probably just a bishop's chair. The two other buildings giving onto the square — *Palazzo dell'Archivio* and *Palazzo del Consiglio* — were built in the 14th century. Today they are a museum, the **Museo dell'Estuario**.